SHOWERS OF BLESSINGS

SHOWERS OF BLESSINGS

Jim Bakker

Dedicated
to
"Our Partners"
from whom Tammy and I
have received the support and strength
for the tasks God has called
us to do.

CONTENTS

SHOWERS OF BLESSINGS

FOREWORD

SUCCESSFUL MEN EXCITE ME. Especially, when they talk about the secrets that changed their lives.

That's why this book, *Showers of Blessings*, will become important to you.

Few men have affected the world as Jim Bakker. Few men in Christianity have brought such mass healing to the bruised and wounded body of Christ. And he has done it against unbelievable opposition, criticism, and attacks. Over and over again, satanic strategies have been foiled, and the skilled and brilliant plans of adversaries have crumbled. And there is a reason for this kind of phenomenal success. *This book reveals the real secret*.

You see, Jim's weapon has always been *love*. And his ammunition is *giving*. This explains why his victories are so consistent, his partners so loyal, the touch of God so evident upon his ministry.

I am totally convinced that the Principle of Sowing and Reaping is the *catalyst* law that determines your happiness, your blessings, and ultimately controls the God-Man relationship. That's why I feel this book is so valuable.

In my personal opinion, this book will do three things for you:

1) *Reconstruct* any negative thinking about giving to the work of God;
2) *Release* the explosive energy within you called FAITH;
3) *Revive* your ability to dream big again.

The greatest thing any man can do for you is to help unlock your faith in God. *Jim does*. He has always unlocked my biggest seeds. Consequently, my biggest blessings! For that, I am eternally grateful.

Keep this book by your bedside. Mark it with your pen. Review it often. And always remember: "WHEN YOU LET GO OF SOMETHING IN YOUR HAND, GOD WILL LET GO OF SOMETHING IN HIS HAND FOR YOU."

Mike Murdock
February 1986

INTRODUCTION

This book is not about theory. It is about results. It is written for your encouragement because I believe the blessings that result from giving are among the best-kept secrets in the body of Christ today.

Over two years ago, the Lord laid on my heart to build the biggest project that our ministry, Heritage Village Church, had ever attempted—a multi-million dollar Partner Center, enabling literally millions of people to come to Heritage USA each year to receive ministry and miracles for their lives and to enjoy fellowship with other Christians from around the world.

Skeptics in and outside the church considered it an impossible venture. The media scoffed at us. I admit that the concept was so immense and revolutionary, I was awed by what God had directed us to do. How could we possibly accomplish this? Would we ask banks to finance it and pay millions of dollars of interest—or would we have to cut our other outreaches and use ministry funds?

While I was praying about all this early one morning, God revealed a way whereby our Partners would share in the benefits, both materially and spiritually, in return for their help in building the new Partner Center. By inviting our viewers to give $1000 to become Lifetime Partners, they would receive a gift of four days and three nights lodging with their family every year in the Partner Center.* I realized this was an idea from God, for as I shared it with our Partners, in just a matter of months, all the memberships in our Heritage Grand Hotel were taken. Demand for lodging in the Partner Center has been so overwhelming, we have added a second phase, the new twenty-one-story Heritage Towers complex.

Something else even more exciting was happening at the same time. As people began to send in their gifts to become Lifetime Partners, we started hearing about dramatic victories in their lives. As they gave to the Lord's work, God began pouring out amazing and unexpected blessings!

Daily, I read miraculous accounts where families that had houses or properties that wouldn't sell for years suddenly sold after they gave. Others had their dream home provided. After giving, people discovered insurance policies and bonds worth thousands of dollars which they never knew existed. People were paid debts years in advance. Lifetime Partners had their business suddenly double, triple, and even increase tenfold. Others

---

*By offering one half of the Partner Center rooms to Lifetime Partners on a first come, first serve space-available basis, occupancy of the other half by paying guests could pay to maintain this Christian lodging facility. Our finance people confirmed this was a viable plan.

had unexpected checks arrive in the mail; people were given new cars, new homes, received healings, had families restored—all kinds of divine blessings.

The reports started out as a trickle, but soon began pouring into my office. I announced to my staff that unless we published these miraculous reports, no one would believe they really happened.

As I prepared to publish this book of testimonies, I discovered that our Partners were simply obeying God's fixed law of giving. This is not a secret formula for success . . . it is God's law and it works. This amazing collection of testimonies proves it.

What is this law? How does it work? How can we receive showers of blessings? That is what this book is about. . . . the principles of God's law, the practical application, and the amazing results. It has turned hundreds of lives around. Let it do the same for you!

1

THE FIXED LAW OF GIVING

I had never expected to write a book on giving—not that I don't have experience on the subject. In our 25 years of gospel ministry, Tammy and I have been privileged to both give and raise many millions of dollars for God's work.

However, much of our involvement has been out of necessity, because I never really enjoyed asking people to give to support our ministry. If there was any other way I could fulfill God's calling to bring the Gospel via television to all nations other than by appealing to our Partners, I would have tried it. The major TV networks have been closed to gospel programming and advertising agencies won't consider selling commercial time for our broadcast. So I am left with raising our multi-million dollar yearly budget with free-will offerings.

My attitude about asking people to give has completely changed. The testimonies contained in this book have gotten me more excited about giving than anything I've read or heard. Through them, I've discovered one of God's greatest laws—the fixed law of giving.

Some of God's universal laws are obvious. We never hear testimonies about God's faithfulness to the law of gravity because it is so obvious. Others of God's laws are just as sure but less apparent.

One such law is God's fixed law of agreement found in Matthew 18:19, "Again, I say unto you, that if two of you shall agree on earth as touching any thing that they shall ask, it shall be done for them of my Father which is in heaven." This has been the theme verse of PTL ever since its beginning. Our ministry has grown on the basis of prayer agreement with our viewers through our 24-hour daily prayer phones.

In one 40-day period when we emphasized prayer agreement, we invited viewers to report their answer to prayer. The result was the publishing of a several hundred page book called *God Answers Prayer*, reporting thousands of miraculous reports of answered prayer.

This testimony book concerns another of God's fixed laws—the law of giving. This law is found in Malachi 3:10,11, "Bring ye all the tithes into the storehouse, that there may be meat in mine house, and prove me now herewith, saith the Lord of hosts, if I will not open you the windows of heaven, and pour you out a blessing, that there shall not be room enough to receive it. And I will rebuke the devourer for your sake, and he shall not destroy the fruits of your ground, neither shall your vine cast her fruit before the time in the field, saith the Lord of hosts."

The fixed law of giving can best be described as the law of sowing and reaping. When we sow (give) to God's work, we reap from God a harvest of blessing. It may be financial, spiritual, or physical—God promises to meet our needs when we give to His work.

God tells the Israelites that He so wants to materially bless them that He says "Prove Me—put Me to the test and see if I won't bless you." This is the only place in the Bible where God says to prove or test Him—that He might perform His promise.

The tithe (ten percent of our income) is just the start or minimum that God commands we sow to reap His blessing. The Old Testament Law declared that the tithe of all land and income was the Lord's (Lev. 27:30). Offerings are that given above the amount of the tithe.

Our Scripture says that when we sow a harvest by giving tithes and offerings, God promises to pour out such a blessing that we won't have room to contain it.

Many people are not being blessed in this way. Why not? Because they are like the Israelites in Malachi 3:8,9, "Will a man rob God? Yet ye have robbed me. But ye say 'Wherein have we robbed thee?' In tithes and offerings. Ye are cursed with a curse, for ye have robbed me, even this whole nation."

The Israelites were robbing God. How? By not giving Him their tithes and offerings. But you say "How can you rob God? He already has everything and doesn't depend on us for help." We can rob God of His opportunity to materially bless us when we don't give.

In not giving, we are cursed with a curse. However, we can break and erase that curse just by beginning to obey God and give. Not only do we break the curse, but we bind the one who does the cursing. God declares in the fixed law of giving that He will rebuke the devourer for our sake.

That means Satan, the thief and robber, cannot steal our blessing or take away the rewards of our labor when we give. God promises that our fruit won't drop in the field before it is ripe, and bugs and pestilence won't come and steal our harvest.

Recently I've had many people ask me, "Jim, what is your secret? How could your ministry grow from a little struggling TV broadcast in a rented furniture store to become one of the largest Christian ministries in the world in just ten years?"

I tell them, "The secret is giving."

When Tammy and I first started PTL, we began to prove God by giving. We gave and gave until we didn't have to give—and still we gave. Whenever I've hit a bump in the road, I'd plant a gift in someone else's vineyard.

With my natural mind, I can't understand this, but the seed I sow to other ministries comes back to grow fruit and blessings in ours. The more I give to help others the more God gives back to me.

In services, people often approach me and say, "Oh, Jim, agree with me in prayer that God will bless me financially."

When I ask them if they are giving, they usually reply, "No, I can't afford to give anything. Pray that God will bless me."

It doesn't work just by prayer. I can't pray in agreement if the person won't obey God's Word.

Oh, they might get a little spurt of God's blessing. But they could have a whole pipeline of blessing. All they have to do is to get into the flow of God by beginning to give their tithes and offerings.

Saint or sinner, God's fixed law of giving produces the same results. I've known many sinners who have tithed and prospered.

You wonder why the heads of major corporations make a lot of money? There is order and fixed principles in God's Kingdom. When you help a lot of people, you get blessed yourself, no matter where you are or what you're doing. When you employ tens of thousands of people with millions and millions of dollars of revenue going back to your employees, you're going to prosper. It's God's Law.

One of the most interesting interviews that Tammy has ever done was with Mr. T, the popular TV and Hollywood movie star. When Tammy asked Mr. T what was the key, the turning point, of success in his acting career, Mr. T replied, "I never dreamed of being an actor. I got picked for the part in "Rocky" out of 15,000 guys who auditioned. I believe I won the part because of God's blessings. The first money that I ever earned as an actor I gave to the church to feed the less fortunate in our community. I've been taught what the Bible says about giving so my blessing came back in the way I believed it would."

You may say, "Well, it's easy for Mr. T to give, but I can't afford to give." The reason Mr. T can now afford to give is because he began giving when he couldn't afford it, either.

The widow of Zarephath in I Kings 17 was sure that she could not afford to give to God's servant when Elijah asked her for a cup of water and a morsel of bread. She said, "We're down to our last meal and then my son and I must die of starvation." But Elijah directed her to give that last loaf out of her need, promising that if she would, "God says that there will always be plenty of flour and oil left in your containers." Not only did God supply her needs as she gave, but her giving qualified her for divine intervention when her son got sick and died. God used Elijah to restore her son back to life. That's double divine benefits!

For years, I have had accountants and advisors who have told me PTL couldn't afford to be giving so much. When our ministry was headquartered in a small rented furniture store, they told me that I couldn't afford to remodel and put a little thousand square foot addition onto it, saying, "Jim, you can't do it. You don't have any money!"

Right then, I decided to plant a seed for God to bless. What could I plant? I didn't have any money, but I did have a car and a mobile home that we weren't using at the time. I gave them away along with some TV equipment. By the time my harvest came in, we built, not that little addition, but rather a totally new multi-million dollar ministry center called Heritage Village, the first permanent headquarters for the PTL ministry.

Our budget has grown from $10,000 to ten million dollars a month and people are still insisting, "Jim, you can't afford to give." And I reply, "I can't afford *not* to give if I want to prosper and be blessed."

I believe that I have the greatest and most blessed

ministry staff in the world. And it's largely because when they come to PTL, they quickly learn to give and expect God's blessing.

Toni Bogart came to PTL to join our music department as one of our Celebration Singers. With the moving expenses, etc., of coming to PTL, Toni was experiencing severe financial problems. It finally came down to either giving her tithe or making her car payment. Having heard me preach from Malachi 3 on the subject of giving, she decided to put God to the test. She wrote out her check for the tithe, placed it in the offering, and then began to trust God for the car payment.

The very next day, Toni received an envelope in the mail with a check enclosed. Says Toni, "I thought it was for $1,000 and was thrilled. But then my roommate said that I had missed a zero. It was for $10,000! My grandmother had established a trust fund in my name and was led to send it to me at that particular time."

Was this a coincidence? If it were just Toni's story alone, we could say "perhaps." But when we add the testimony of hundreds of others in this book proving God's faithfulness, we must acknowledge "No". Rather, this is God's fixed law of giving at work.

God has a harvest of blessings just waiting for you. The seed you plant in God's work will determine just how bountiful your harvest will be.

2

RELEASING GOD'S BLESSINGS

In Luke 6:38, Jesus repeats the fixed law of giving and reveals more clearly the secret of releasing God's blessings when He says, "Give, and it shall be given unto you, good measure, pressed down, and shaken together and running over, shall men give into your bosom. For with the same measure that ye mete withal, it shall be measured to you again."

This verse contains several key principles of God's fixed law of giving. Already, we've learned that God wants to bless us materially. Now Jesus adds the promise that our return in blessings will be greater than our giving and only limited by the amount we give, whether large or small.

Not long ago, the Lord gave Tammy a beautiful vision of this principle. She saw in the Spirit a great river much like the one in Minnesota that her uncle worked as a logger. However, this river was filled with God's blessings—finances, new homes, new cars, healing streams, all kinds of divine provision. Unfortunately, most all of the blessings were log-jammed together and weren't getting to the people who needed them. Then God spoke to Tammy and said, "The only way to break this logjam and loose the blessings is for the people to give."

By giving our viewers the opportunity to get involved in building the Partner Center with their Lifetime Partnerships, we have had a great increase in giving. Many Partners have given with great sacrifice. What were the results? Instead of hearing of people struggling and failing and doing without, reports of blessings, miracles, and unexpected prosperity began flooding my office, and have never stopped.

What was really amazing to me was how soon the divine blessings followed our Partners' giving. For so many, it was the same day or week. People like the Bruce Binkemeier family of Lake Oswego, Oregon, who sent $1,000 to become Lifetime Partners. The very next day, their realtor called to say that a building they had up for sale for years had suddenly sold for $120,000 cash.

This report and hundreds just like it convinces me that God has a multitude of blessings ready to be released to us as soon as we begin to give.

Another amazing thing was the size of God's blessings in return. When someone sends $1,000 to support our worldwide ministry and become a Lifetime Partner, he or she has the potential of receiving in return several thousands of dollars value in free lodging at our Partner Center. Yet above all this, many of our Lifetime Partners have experienced additional material blessings from the Lord.

God's promise is, "Give and it shall be given unto you, pressed down, shaken together, and running over . . ." This means more, bigger, and better. When I think of "pressed down," my mind immediately returns to Mills' Ice Cream Store in Muskegon, Michigan, where we always went as kids.

I loved to watch the man at the counter serve hand-packed ice cream. He would take that big scoop and pack and pack the ice cream into the container. Then he'd pound it down and pack in some more. Just when you thought the container couldn't possibly hold any more, he'd squeeze in one more mound of ice cream on top. That's exactly the way the Lord blesses our giving—pressed down, shaken together, and running over.

The next part of our verse says ". . . shall men give unto your bosom." God uses people to give His divine blessings. Now, you mustn't think that the person or ministry to whom you gave your gift is necessarily going to give back to you. If that happened, they'd be your source and pretty soon you'd be running down to the local bank, saying, "Here's a big donation. I know you've got lots of money, so I know it will come back to me."

I've learned that you might just as likely get kicked as get blessed by the people to whom you give. People that have hurt me the most are some that I've helped out of the deepest pits. It has happened enough to almost tempt me to stop helping people. The devil would whisper in my ear, "See, you gave to that person and now he's stolen from you or is out spreading lies. So why help people?"

I don't understand it all but the Lord has enabled me not to become bitter. Perhaps, God allowed these people to turn on me so that I would realize they couldn't be my source. God has made me see that He alone is my source. He will use whosoever He chooses to "give unto your *bosom*."

The word "bosom" is more accurately translated in the New International Version as "lap." In Bible days, people wore great flowing robes with large folds of material draped over their shoulder. In the lap of these robes, they could carry a great abundance.

It reminds me of my Grandmother Irwin's big apron. She'd go out to pick tomatoes in the garden and would bring back what seemed to be a bushelful in that big apron—so much more than she could have carried in her hands. This was the principle Jesus was illustrating here—when you give, you are going to have so much, you won't be able to hold it in your hands. It will fill your lap to overflowing.

This enables us to continue the cycle of giving. God always gives back to us an overflowing measure so we can give again—and more. Paul declared this truth to the believers in Corinth: "God, who gives seed to the farmer to plant and later on, good crops to harvest and eat, will give you more and more seed to plant and will make it grow so that you can give away more and more fruit from your harvest. Yes, God will give you so much that you can give away much. . . ." (2 Cor. 9:10,11 Living Bible).

Solomon declared much the same truth in Proverbs 11:24,25: "It is possible to give away and become richer! It is also possible to hold on too tightly and lose everything. Yes, the liberal men shall be rich! By watering others, he waters himself."

The reason God gives us an abundant supply is so that we won't be tempted to hold onto our blessing in our tight little hands, blocking the continued flow that God desires.

What measure does God use to pour His blessings back to us? That depends on the measure we use to give. The Living Bible translates the second half of our verse in Luke 6:38, "Whatever measure you use to give—large or small—will be used to measure what is given back to you."

There is the familiar story of the general store keeper who went to the baker and complained, "You've been cheating me. I weighed that pound of bread I bought from you and it was ounces short."

The baker replied, "Oh, really! I was just using the pound of cornmeal I bought at your store as a counterweight for the pound of bread."

We cheat ourselves when we cheat God by not giving. God uses the same measuring portion that we use to give to Him to give back to us.

I was able to graphically illustrate this truth in a sermon at our Heritage Village Church. First, I took a "change" offering for our Heritage House (home for women in crisis pregnancy). Then, with the help of several deacons, I poured these several hundred pounds of coins into a pile before the congregation.

Getting a little teaspoon, I pointed out that this is the measure some people use to give to God. They say, "God, here is a quarter." Then they wonder why God doesn't bless them. But God must use the same measure they do in giving.

Then there are those that have "oneness" faith. They give one dollar bills in the offering. That, perhaps, deserves a bigger spoon. Still, with that tremendous pile of coins, even a big tablespoon could hold so few. A coffee mug could hold some more and a tall iced tea glass even more, but still very little compared to the huge stack of money.

If I really wanted to make a dent in that "blessing pile," I would need to get a bigger measure—something like that wide and deep coal shovel I found at our Heritage Farm. With just one shovel full, I was able to fill the lap of the robe of one of our choir members.

Remember, God wants us to prove Him. If we give little, God is limited to use a little measure in return. But if we put God to the test in our giving with a large measure like our Lifetime Partners have done, we will experience great showers of blessings, overflowing from our hands and laps to others.

In Galatians 6:7 we read, "Be not deceived, God is not mocked; for whatever a man soweth, that shall he also reap."

In the law of sowing and reaping, when you sow tomatoes, you reap tomatoes; when you sow fleshly lust and greed, you reap corruption; when you sow blessing, you reap even greater blessing. II Corinthians 9:6 says, "He which soweth sparingly shall reap also sparingly; and he which soweth bountifully shall reap also bountifully."

God has a river of blessing prepared for you.

Don't limit Him to a trickle when He wants to shower and overflow you with goodness.

Over the years, our ministry has planted millions of dollars of seed in other ministries. But two and a half years ago, we planted the largest seed in our history when we gave our Canton, Ohio TV station (valued at ten million dollars) to another ministry. We got out the "coal shovel" measure with that offering!

Do you know what God did? Right after that, God gave me the hundred million dollar idea for the Lifetime Partnerships. How much is an idea like that worth? In each of the last two years, God has given us twice as much income as we ever had before. I'd say that is a bountiful harvest!

You probably don't have ten million dollars to plant as seed. But you do have something. It may be a dollar or a thousand dollars. Even if you have no money at all, you can give some clothes to a needy person or a helping hand to a neighbor. Get started giving. You'll be breaking up the devil's log-jam to your blessing and get that overflowing harvest on its way to you!

3

GETTING STARTED GIVING

On our television program recently, evangelist Mike Murdock told me something very powerful when he said, "Jim, you don't have to create or perform the miracle you need; you just need to get it started. God will do the rest."

Over and over in the Bible, we see God encouraging people to step out in faith to get their miracle going. Then He took over. Mathematics tells us that zero multiplied by a million times is still zero. All of God's power, all of His provision, is still nil until we give Him something with which to work.

The widow of Zarephath had to give the prophet her last meal cake in order to loose God's miracle supply; Moses had to lift the rod; Joshua had to march around Jericho; Naaman had to wash in Jordan; and Jesus needed the lad's lunch of five loaves and two fishes before He could multiply the food to feed the ten thousand.

If you, too, want to see a miraculous abundance in your life, you must first give God something to bless and multiply.

Many times I have been criticized for allowing elderly folks on fixed incomes to sacrificially give to support PTL. The secular press complains, "These people can't afford to give to you." I guess they would have had a heyday in criticizing Elijah for eating the widow's cake or condemning Jesus for taking a little boy's lunch.

You know, I was nearly the same way, early in my ministry. It took me years to become a real giver. I had very spiritual excuses for not giving. I said, "My whole life and work is God's; I don't need to give money." The person I cheated in not giving was myself.

Do you know when I was convinced that I had to start giving? It was when I could least afford it. We were really struggling to get PTL started and it looked like we were going to go under. I saw clearly that God was our only hope and He had directed in Scripture that the way out of poverty and lack was by giving.

When I obeyed by giving that car and mobile home, a joy and an expectancy of blessing was quickened in my heart and it has remained there ever since. It was as if a spirit or mindset of poverty were broken which loosed a new dimension of faith and joy.

It has been the same way for Tammy. Until a few years ago, Tammy was not a big giver. Back then, the financial pressures of the ministry would weigh down on her terribly. Then Tammy began to give—not just her tithe but great offerings above her tithe.

Now she's become one of the top givers in our ministry. Tammy is always giving of what she has and God keeps blessing her back with more. But the real blessing is that she is now caught up with God's goodness instead of ministry financial troubles.

Both Tammy and I have discovered that whenever the ministry or one of our projects gets in a deep financial bind, we can give our way out of that bind. Just recently, our Fort Hope project (for shelter and rehabilitation of street people) was really struggling and almost came to a complete stop because of lack of finances. We decided to "attack the lack" by donating to this project a beautiful antique car (replica of a 1928 Mercedes) I'd been given. Pretty soon, people and companies all around the nation were donating materials, support, and labor. Over a quarter million dollars was raised in a charity auction to help build this much needed center.

In II Corinthians 8, the Bible records that the Macedonian churches discovered this same secret. Paul writes in verses 2–4, "Though they have been going through much trouble and hard times, they have mixed their wonderful joy with their deep poverty, and the result has been an overflow of giving to others. They gave not only what they could afford, but far more, and I can testify that they did it because they wanted to, and not because of nagging on my part. They begged us to take the money so they could share in the joy of helping the Christians in Jerusalem."

How did the churches in Macedonia get started giving?

First, they gave sacrificially, in a way that

stretched their faith. For some, that might have been a widow's mite; for others, it was much more. Give at your level of faith.

When Tammy and I were traveling evangelists, living from day to day, it was every bit as challenging to put that last twenty dollar bill in the offering and believe God would supply the next meal, as it has been to donate millions of dollars through PTL. Because we proved God and He never failed us at the twenty dollar level, our faith has grown so that we give more and more.

Second, the Macedonians saw the need and gave their best. They didn't give their leftovers or second-hand goods. They rallied the best they had, to give to others.

Don't give your junk to God. The prophet Malachi had to chastise the Israelites for doing this. Instead of offering to God their best lambs, they were bringing Him their blind and sickly ones (Mal. 1:7). For this reason, God was refusing and ignoring their sacrifices (vs. 10–14), so the people weren't being blessed.

Give to God your best—and that same joy and expectancy that filled the Macedonians will fill your heart and carry you on to victory.

Third, they didn't just pledge to give. Despite adverse conditions, they followed through to give what they had promised. In this way, they were different from the church at Corinth, who had to be admonished by Paul, "I want to suggest that you finish what you started to do a year ago, for you were not only the first to propose this idea [helping the Christians at Jerusalem], but the first to begin doing something about it. Having started the ball rolling so enthusiastically, you should carry this project through to completion just as gladly giving whatever you can, out of whatever you have. Let your enthusiastic idea at the start be equalled by your realistic action now" (II Cor. 8:10,11).

So many people are like the church at Corinth— robbed of blessings because they don't follow through on their pledge to give. At PTL, we've found that among those pledging to give for twelve months, we only receive an average three or four monthly gifts. If everyone paid their monthly pledges faithfully, we would never have to raise money on the air other than on our yearly telethon.

Though our ministry suffers when people don't follow through in giving, the people who pledge and then fail to, suffer more. They are actually allowing the devil rob them of their seed just as Jesus described in the parable of the sower in Matthew 13. How much better for the church at Corinth, for our PTL Partners, and perhaps for you, if everyone would follow through to plant their seed and receive a thirty-, sixty-, or hundredfold return on their giving (Matt. 13:8).

Fourth, the Macedonian church gave joyfully and cheerfully. God loves a cheerful giver (II Cor. 9:7). We cannot really give cheerfully if we aren't expecting a blessing in return.

God wants you to begin giving in the same way as the Macedonians. Give so your faith will be stretched in proving God at whatever level you can give. Follow through and give cheerfully and expectantly. As Paul encouraged the church at Corinth, "If you are really eager to give, then it isn't important how much you have to give. God wants you to give what you have, not what you haven't" (II Cor. 8:12).

Steve Rhoads, another of our PTL Singers, was in this position soon after coming to the ministry. He had been saving a little money to repair his old car or to try and get a better one. Knowing that the $100 he had saved wasn't enough to do either, he decided to prove God and give the money he'd saved to PTL.

The week Steve gave his offering, his car roof collapsed and then the engine died. It looked like his giving had backfired. Yet he didn't give up his faith. He went out and started to look for a new car.

The next day, Steve's parents called to tell him about an old bank account that his grandfather had opened in his name. To Steve's amazement, it now had accrued to $10,000.

Through another miraculous set of circumstances, Steve was able to find his brand-new "dream" car at a three thousand dollar discount. The total price was $10,000.53, so Steve's new car cost 53¢ and one act of obedient giving to God.

Steve needed a miracle with his car. He couldn't bring it about himself, but he got it started by giving to God all he had to work with. Then God took over.

He will do the same for you if you start giving.

If you feel bound by your lack today, let's break that bondage by finding something good that you can give so that God can begin blessing you.

4

HOW TO GET YOUR MIRACLE

If anyone in this world is qualified to speak about divine miracles, perhaps it is Tammy and myself. It is not at all that we have any special kind of faith, it is because our entire twenty-five years of ministry have been spent pioneering work for the Lord in situations where we have had to depend totally on Him. In fact, in our eleven years with PTL, the ministry has grown to the place where we've needed a miracle almost every day.

Recently, some pastors felt led to give me some "encouragement." They were advising me to slow down and not try to do so much. They said, "Jim, you know, it seems like your ministry is on the brink of disaster just about all the time."

I replied, "Well, I guess that depends on how you look at things. I prefer to see that we're constantly on the brink of God's miracles."

Some of you who are reading this book think that your finances, your family, your very lives, are on the brink of disaster. But really, you are on the brink of a miracle. And I want to tell you how to receive that miracle.

Now, I'm not one to spout easy, guaranteed solutions or perfect formulas, but God's Word is just as true today as it was when it was written. The same truths that worked for Jesus' disciples will work for you and me.

I believe this message is so valuable that I suggest you open your Bible as you read this chapter. Mark the passages and write the principles beside the verses shared.

Turn to Mark 6:35–44, and write in the upper margin: How To Receive Your Miracle. In verse 35, the disciples were in a position to really need a miracle—not just for themselves but also for the 10,000 or more people with them who had come out to this desert place to receive Jesus' teaching. It had been at least one long day, and possibly two or three. Everyone was hungry and needed to be fed.

So the disciples did what everyone who wants a miracle should do: *They admitted they had a need.* They went to Jesus with their problem saying, "This is a desert place and now the time is far passed. Send them [the crowd] away, that they may go . . . buy themselves bread, for they have nothing to eat."

The disciples recognized and admitted their need. We all must realize it's not a sin to say that we have a need. In fact, the Bible says you have not because you don't ask (James 4:3). We have Christians who go around saying, "Don't ever say anything negative; never confess you're sick or in need." Hogwash! If you're sick, you're sick! You can't con or play mind games with God. Our loving Father wants us to say, "God, I have a need."

What if your child came up to you and said, "Daddy, I've got all the jelly beans I need. I don't

40

want any more jelly beans." Are you going to give him any? Of course not.

But if he comes and says, "Daddy, please give me some jelly beans. I'm so hungry for jelly beans and haven't had any for so long. Please, daddy, PLEASE?" Even though jelly beans aren't good for his teeth or tummy or anything else, you'll probably wind up giving him jelly beans because you love him and he's pleading with you.

The Bible says we are God's children and He wants us to be like little children. We are to go to him like children, admitting our needs and asking His help. Our marriage workshop counselors say the hardest hurdle to cross in healing marriages is to get the couples to admit their need. Sometimes our counselors have to dig for days to get the couple to recognize their need. When it happens, something inside them breaks and they are set free to be healed and delivered. The first step in acknowledging our need is crucial.

When the disciples told Jesus the multitude needed food, He said to them, "Give ye them to eat . . . How many loaves have ye? go and see. And when they knew, they said, Five, and two fishes!" (vs. 37, 38). This is the second step in getting your miracle. Find out what you can do about your need, just as the disciples began to look and seek for resources to help. As we discussed in the last chapter, start giving and doing something. *Begin to do what you can do*.

If you're going to build a house or buy a home, you're going to go look, and scrape together a down payment. Then you say, "God, help me to find a house to buy with this much down payment." Get whatever you can together and you will be well on your way to your miracle.

The disciples gathered all the available resources but they still weren't quite ready for the miracle. For the Lord "commanded them to make all sit down by companies . . . in ranks by hundreds and fifties" (vs. 39, 40). *They prepared for the miracle.*

They exercised their faith to organize, to prepare for the miracle to happen. Why have I built this great Partner Center? Because I believe the Lord is going to fill it with people who will be ministered to by His Spirit in this place.

When they were prepared, Jesus took the five loaves and the two fishes and offering them to heaven, blessed and brake them (vs. 41). This is the next key: *Thank God for what you've got.* Whatever you have, no matter how small, be thankful for it. Don't complain. You will wander in the desert for 40 years like the Israelites if you grumble and bemoan your situation.

Jesus didn't just thank God for what little he had, He began to *give it away.* That's when the miracle really began to happen. This is when your miracle will happen, too—when you give what you have. You say, "What can I give? I've only got 29 cents." Give your 29 cents. Don't worry if the need is a million dollars. If five loaves and two fishes could feed more than 10,000 people until all did eat and were filled (vs. 42), then God can use and multiply whatever you have to meet whatever need there is.

The little boy with the five loaves and two fish could have easily thought, "What is my little lunch going to do for the need of this great big crowd?" You might be thinking the same thing when you look at your resources and needs.

When PTL was in its infancy, it was easy for people to see how their ten or fifteen dollar monthly gift would help keep our program on the air in their area and support our little staff in the rented furniture store. As we've grown, however, building larger facilities, increasing our staff, and carrying our outreaches to the ends of the earth, it is tempting for people to think, "PTL is so big. What possible difference could my little gift make? So why send it?"

Actually, we receive very, very few large gifts. From surveys, I know that we are viewed by many, many wealthy people, so I've been surprised that so few support us to any great degree. Sadly, many today are like the rich young ruler of old, trusting in their own wealth. The Apostle Paul warns Timothy that this is a great stumbling block: "Tell those who are rich not to be proud and not to trust in their money, which will soon be gone, but their pride and trust should be in the living God who always richly gives us all we need for our enjoyment. Tell them to use their money to do good. They should be rich in good works and should give happily to those in need, always being ready to share with others whatever God has given them. By doing this, they will be storing up real treasure for themselves in heaven." (I Tim. 6:17–19).

This is good advice for all of us. However, we

will always be dependent on our faithful ten and fifteen dollar monthly givers. These are the people who make our ministry happen. We operate almost entirely on these small, faithful gifts, and when our monthly giving drops, it cripples the entire ministry.

So never think that your little is too little to be important. What a blessing it must have been to that young lad to see his "miracle" loaves and fish feeding those 10,000-plus people. Actually, I believe that everyone there got to participate in the miracle. Verse 41 says the bread and fish "divided he among them all." I can just picture each person receiving a piece of bread or fish and dividing it as a piece for himself and one for his neighbor. Each time it was divided it grew and multiplied. This is the miracle of giving—it blesses others besides yourself.

Perhaps the greatest miracle, though, is the *running over* in verse 43, "And afterwards, they took up twelve baskets full of the fragments, and of the fishes." Not only did they have enough to fill everyone, but everyone could bring a bag of leftovers home and then they could also share with the poor, lepers, and orphans.

God always gives us more than we need so we can give to Him and others. The only way we stop God's blessing is when we devour our extra seed and stop the flow of planting and harvesting.

The worldly, natural mind can not understand that the way to receive more is to give more. The way out of poverty to prosperity is through giving.

Does it really work? The patriarch Abraham says

yes as he receives the blessing of Melchizedek (Gen. 14:19); yes, says his son Isaac as he receives a hundredfold return (Gen. 26:12); the widow of Zarepheth says yes with her miraculous supply (I Kings 17); Job says yes as the Lord blessed the latter end of Job (Job 42:12). King David says yes (Ps. 30:6); King Solomon says yes (Prov. 11:24); the prophets Isaiah (Isa. 58:7, 8), Daniel (Dan. 6:28), and Malachi say yes; Jesus says yes (Luke 6:38); the apostle Paul says yes (II Cor. 8), James says yes (James 2:5); Tammy and I say yes; and all the Partner testimonies in this book declare a loud yes.

You, too, can say yes. Acknowledge your need to God, begin to gather your resources, prepare for a miracle, thank God for what you have, and then give. A miracle is on its way.

5

FRUITFULNESS, THE HUNDREDFOLD BLESSING

During our recent period of growth and Partner giving, God has been emphasizing one particular number over and over to me—the number nine. During one on-location program, when it looked like several of our projects, including the Partner Center, were going to have to stop and possibly even fail, nine ducks flew in a direct line and landed on the lake right in front of us.

Soon afterwards the Lord called my attention to a beautiful painting of birds—nine of them. This happened again and again. So I asked the Lord to reveal its meaning. He led me to a Bible commentary where I learned that *nine* was the number of fruitfulness. Was God bringing forth fruitfulness in our ministry?

I found myself saying, "Yes, Lord, I receive that for our ministry." Hadn't our world missions outreach grown as never before? One missions expert had estimated that PTL could now touch one billion lives worldwide.

At home, our more than 800 People That Love Centers were helping to feed and clothe millions of people; over 7,000 volunteers were reaching out in over 1,000 jails and prisons across America; our home for women in crisis pregnancy was working to stem abortion and other such homes would soon be established; thousands of marriages were being saved through our workshop ministry; Heritage USA had become the third most-visited attraction in America; and now the new Partner Center enables millions of people to come and stay at Heritage USA for more ministry and spiritual growth.

The Lord convicted me that He wanted to do more than just make PTL fruitful. He wanted the Partners to be fruitful, too.

How does one become fruitful? The Bible says it is by planting seed in good soil: "But other [seed] fell into good ground, and brought forth fruit, some one hundredfold, some sixtyfold, some thirtyfold" (Matt. 13:8).

Is an hundredfold return on the seed we plant really possible? In the Gospel of Mark, Chapter 10, Verses 29 and 30, Jesus declares: "There is no man that hath left [given] house, or brethren or sisters, or father or mother or wife, or children or land for my sake, and the gospel's, but he shall receive *an hundredfold now in this time houses and brethren and sisters and mothers and children and lands with persecutions; and in the world to come eternal life."*

Yes, an hundredfold blessing is possible for us, for our families, in our jobs, and in eternal life. This has been very much a reality in our ministry. Soon after we began to actively apply God's fixed law of giving, we had an independent auditing firm evaluate all the areas of our ministry. Their investigation documented that in one year, PTL's rate of growth was measured at a whopping 7,000 percent!

Interestingly enough, this growth occurred during a period when we were going through great persecution from the media, government, and others—just as the above Scripture warns. (Notice that verse 29 says "left" or "given up.") More than once I have had to put the whole PTL ministry on the altar and give it all back to God. The Lord in return has blessed us back an hundredfold.

More recently, a horrendous problem in our mailing system caused us to lose many of our regular supporters and resulted in our falling millions of dollars behind in our bills. We needed a miracle desperately!

On this particular day, the wife of a precious local pastor friend sat in our program audience. As I stood to address them after the program, God spoke to my heart and said, "If you want your debts paid, you need to plant seed for a ten million dollar harvest [that was the amount of our debt]. So give this local church $100,000."

When I obeyed, this pastor's wife almost fainted. She told me that at that very moment, her husband was out trying to beg or borrow $100,000 to keep the church from bankruptcy.

What happened to our seed? That month, we received nine million dollars, the largest month of giving in our history up to that time. We received a hundredfold return in just five weeks.

The Bible tells us in Genesis 26:12 that Isaac also received a hundredfold blessing: "Then Isaac sowed in the land and received in the same year an hundredfold: and the Lord blessed him." Abraham had placed Isaac on the altar in total obedience and surrender to God. The result? A hundredfold blessing in Isaac's life.

At our Heritage Village Church worship services, we see the offering time as an integral part of our worship and yielding to God. When we make the announcement to prepare for the offering, the congregation loudly applauds. This is another opportunity for giving.

Our people rejoice that they can give; they know what is going to happen. God is going to meet and bless them. As their pastor, their clapping reminds me of God's blessing and I remember to pray and ask God for a hundredfold return on their tithes and offerings.

This new attitude toward giving is working wonders! More members of our church have been able to move into their own homes than ever before. God is blessing others with new cars and still others with healings, salvation of loved ones, and restoration of family members. What value can you possibly place on these wonderful gifts from God?

God is not just making our local church members fruitful but rather all of our PTL Partners. Not long ago we took a survey of the income of our PTL Partners (those who regularly support our ministry). Not only did we find that it ($36,000) averaged nearly twice the income of the average American, but that it had risen by over 20% in less than two years.

This is God's faithfulness at work, bringing forth

fruit through our Partners' giving to God's ministry.

Like the Apostle Paul with the church at Philippi, I rejoice in our Partners' giving, "Not because I desire a gift; but I desire fruit that may abound to your account" (Phil. 4:17). I know like Paul that through this giving, "My God shall supply all your need according to his riches in glory by Christ Jesus" (Phil. 4:19).

That is fruitfulness! Our needs are met by God's riches when we give.

6

MORE THAN MONEY: HEALTH, SUCCESS, & FORGIVENESS

Giving can and should involve much more than giving money. The "measure" principle (the measure we use to give will be used to give back to us) of the fixed law of giving applies to nearly every area of life.

One thing that we as Christians must learn to give liberally is kindness. The Bible tells us that "whenever we can we should always be kind of everyone, and especially to our Christian brothers" (Gal. 6:10).

I have known of waitresses and hairdressers—people who depend on tips for their livelihood—becoming discouraged by the lack of kindness and generosity shown by their patrons, even Christians.

How disheartening! What a poor testimony! We Christians with the fruit of the Holy Spirit ought to be the most generous. Instead, how often with our Christian brothers and sisters, we try to scrimp by or even take advantage of one another's goodness.

Kindness costs so little extra but so often, we just don't take the little extra time and effort to do it and it would mean so much to the Lord and others if we did. Despite being criticized for doing so, I've always tried to send a thank-you gift to my Partners for their gifts to PTL. Certainly, nearly all of our Partners would still support PTL without my giving them a Bible or record or book. However, it costs me so little extra to be kind to them in this way. I want our ministry to be an example to Christians in every way.

One area where kindness often is neglected is with the poor. Yet this is where we can receive our greatest blessing. The Bible gives us these wonderful promises in Psalm 41, Verses 1–3, "God blesses those who are kind to the poor. He helps them out of their troubles. He protects them and keeps them alive; he publicly honors them and destroys the power of their enemies. He nurses them when they are sick and soothes their pains and worries."

Those wonderful promises alone are enough to make me want to help the poor. Our Love Centers across this nation are now feeding and clothing millions of needy folks every year. When I am threatened by some troubles our ministry is facing, I am reminded of what all we are doing for the poor and am assured that the Lord will bring us through.

Do you want the best insurance possible? Do you want healing? Do you want public honors? Do you want to be free from worries, enemies, and oppression? The answer is simple. Get involved in giving and helping the poor.

Another area where we all need to express our giving is in *forgiving*. Jesus tells us in Matthew 7:1,

2, "Judge not, that ye be not judged. For with what judgement ye judge, ye shall be judged: and with what measure ye mete, it shall be measured to you again."

One of the greatest and most rewarding gifts you can give yourself is the forgiveness of others. Unforgiveness is one luxury you cannot afford to be living with.

Through 25 years of ministry, I have had many people hurt and abuse me, mostly Christian brothers and sisters. On more than one occasion, fellow workers have attempted to or have actually taken over ministries that Tammy and I had started or raised up with God's help. But early in our ministry we learned that to hold hatred or unforgiveness in our hearts only wound up hurting us. When we released them to the Lord in forgiveness, God always blessed us with something better in ministry. And God always took care of the other person, too.

Doctors and psychologists tell us that holding bitterness and unforgiveness is one of the quickest ways to destroy one's own health. One psychiatrist claims that over 90% of all sickness is related to bitterness and unforgiveness and that it is the root of nearly all mental problems.

In Dr. McMillian's book, *None of These Diseases*, he cites 51 diseases which are caused by emotional stress and unforgiveness.

I'll never forget a lady I met who was all gnarled up and crippled. She was actually a very beautiful lady—and not very old—but she looked like she was a hundred! Her pastor told me her husband had hurt her and now she hated him. She had said, "I would rather *die* than forgive him for what he did to me."

What a price to pay! Unforgiveness, above all, blocks God's flow of forgiveness to us. Without His forgiveness, none of us can reach heaven or have eternal life.

A third area where we need to give for our own sakes and others' is to give *mercy*. Jesus declared this in the Sermon on the Mount when He said, "Blessed are the merciful for they shall obtain mercy" (Matt. 5:7).

I have heard people say "We need more prophets like Jonah." I beg to differ but that is exactly what we don't need. Jonah rebelled against bringing God's message of repentance to Nineveh because he knew they would repent and God would show mercy. When Jonah finally obeyed and the people repented, Jonah pouted because God had mercy on the people.

It is easy to curse or want to bring judgment on people doing wrong. God is looking for people that have His heart, that love mercy, and want to offer grace and help to the hurting and downtrodden.

Why do we need to be tender-hearted and show mercy to others? Because we are certain to need mercy from someone else sooner or later.

The Lord has enabled us at PTL to extend hands of mercy to many types of hurting people. Our prison ministry reaches out to bring hope to so many lost and hopeless people; our New Vine fellowships offer love and deliverance to those trapped in substance abuse; our Love Centers freely provide food and clothing without question or shame; our Opportunity Farm provides shelter and rehabilitation to the homeless; and our home for women in crisis pregnancy offers a Christian life-changing solution to the problem of abortion.

Some of the most touching letters I've received have been from people who, with their giving, have helped us extend a hand of mercy not *knowing* that someday they would need that same miracle of mercy for their own family.

Two years ago, we were building the Heritage House. This ministry touched the heart of Joan Stewart of La Crescenta, California, and she sent in $100 to help rescue babies from abortion.

The Lord spoke to Joan and said, "If you send in the money, you will save a life." Joan thought it was unusual that the Lord said "a life" and not "many lives." She never dreamed at that very moment her own nineteen year-old daughter was in a crisis pregnancy situation and was contemplating having an abortion.

A couple of weeks later, she confided her situation to her mother, saying that she would continue her pregnancy, that God had put faith in her heart to make it.

Because of Joan's mercy, she now has a beautiful granddaughter and a daughter learning to love God. This has happened again and again—to people like Betty Talbert of Minneapolis, Minnesota. As a single parent, she had struggled with raising her son, seeing him lost to alcohol and drug abuse for 13 years.

When Betty saw what we were doing to help addicts and street people, her own "hurting heart" went out to help others and she sent a gift of $1,000 to PTL. When she did this, her son contacted her, said he was at his lowest point, and needed help.

Betty told her son to apply for admittance to the PTL Opportunity Farm. He came, was completely delivered from drugs, committed his life to Christ, is working, and is learning to become a responsible person and loving Christian son. Betty says, "This is the best gift God has ever given us." It all started with Betty showing mercy and giving a gift of love to help others.

The rewards of giving ourselves, in every way through kindness, forgiveness, and mercy, are so great. Begin today to look for more opportunities to give love to others. Remember, as we do unto others, we do unto Christ!

7

GIVE GOD YOUR "HAVE NOTS"

There's a song our PTL Singers sing that says "I'm Yours, Lord, Everything I Am, Everything I'm Not." It talks about giving to God one of the things we all find difficult to do—giving Him our shortcomings and weaknesses.

In my experience, I know I'm not alone when I say that I used to worry a lot more about what I *couldn't do* than what I *could do*. I was more concerned about what I *didn't* have than what I *did have*. That kind of thinking and worrying can really get you down. It is so destructive because *fear of failure can keep you from even trying to accomplish anything*.

I've finally learned that you can give the Lord your *have nots*, just as easily as you can give Him your abilities. When you feel like you've failed and messed up your life, you can give that to the Lord, too.

The good news of the Gospel is that we all start out in life with some handicap or other (Rom. 3:32). These will either become stumbling blocks or stepping stones, depending on whether or not we learn to be overcomers by giving them to God.

Many of the greatest Gospel songs ever written

have been composed by men and women who have endured terribly crushing experiences, but have found God's grace through the valleys and winters of their lives.

I think of the great writer Professor Dorsey, who came and graced our program and whose music has blessed millions. One day he got word on the telephone that his wife had died in childbirth. When he rushed home, lying in the coffin with his wife, was his newborn baby, too. All the words of friends could not comfort him until someone said, "Professor Dorsey, take the hand of Jesus."

Through his tears, he began to write and sing that beloved song, "Precious Lord, take my hand, lead me on, let me stand."

Men do not arrive because the way is made smooth for them. They arrive with God's help, giving Him their fears and failures, handicaps, and shortcomings. Defeat or victory is mainly an inside job—how we deal with what we have and have not.

Check the history books of the world's honor roll—Julius Caesar, Alexander the Great, Socrates—all these suffered with epilepsy before there was any treatment whatever. Catherine the Great of Russia was so deformed as a child, she had to wear braces up and down her body day and night. She was 26 years old before her skull grew together.

Consider the world's great authors. One of the greatest American writers, Robert Louis Stevenson, was considered too sickly to even live. His life was a succession of colds, congestion, hemorrhages, and sinking spells in which he lost the power of speech. Lord Byron and Sir Walter Scott went through life on club feet. Alexander Polk was so much an invalid, he had to be sewn up in canvas before he could stand. Milton and Homer were blind, as was William Prescott, who wrote the *History of The Conquest of Mexico* without ever seeing the paper on which he was writing.

When Browning wrote his first poem, the critics declared "froth, foam, nonsense, trash, balderdash." They told Louisa May Alcott, author of *Little Women*, to stick to sewing instead of writing.

The great scientist, Louis Pasteur, was rated poor to mediocre in chemistry by his teachers. Teachers told Thomas Edison that he was too stupid to learn anything. Walt Disney was discharged from his newspaper job for having "no new good ideas."

Before discovering both the North and South Poles, Admiral Byrd had been dismissed from the Navy for being physically unfit. Abraham Lincoln entered the Black Hawk War a captain and came out a private. His whole life was one of failure, before becoming one of our greatest Presidents. Franklin D. Roosevelt, was a polio victim, yet went down in history as one of our great presidents.

I could go on and on, but handicaps are the common heritage of humanity. We've talked about a lot of success stories but they are not all that way. I could tell you of as many people who died just before they reached their goal or dream or safety. They gave up in the snow just before they reached safety and a warm fire. They dreamed of discovering gold and diamonds and died without discovering that rich vein on their own property. Others turned around just before reaching their dream.

What is the difference between the overcomers and the losers? The losers just gave up and the overcomers refused to give up or only gave everything up to God to see His power take over in victory.

One of Scripture's greatest examples of this is the Apostle Paul, who when he was buffeted by Satan, prayed and found God's strength made perfect in his own weakness. So much so that he declared, "I am glad to be a living demonstration of Christ's power, instead of showing off my own power and abilities. Since I know it is all for Christ's good, I am quite happy about the thorn, and about insults and hardships, persecutions and difficulties; for when I am weak then I am strong—the less I have, the more I depend on Him." (II Cor. 12:10).

Personally, I used to feel like Moses, and say that I couldn't speak. I was too bashful. Yet God called me to speak. As I've given Him my weakness, God has given me His strength. Now I feel His power working through me when I speak.

Tammy felt the same way about her music, that she could never really sing or play the piano. But she gave her voice to Jesus and He has allowed her to bless millions through her music and receive recognition as the number one female Gospel singer in 1984.

It's been said that God is not as concerned about our *ability* as He is about our *availability*. Determine to make your stumbling blocks a stepping stone.

Turn your mistakes into miracles. As Robert Schuller says, "turn your *scars* into *stars*."

The principle of sowing and reaping applies as much to our abilities as it does to our money. Give God what you think you have and what you think you haven't. Little is much with our great God!

8

It Matters Where You Give

Nearly everyone has heard the old saying, "It doesn't matter what you believe as long as you believe in God." That, of course, is a lie. You must study and apply God's Word and guard your belief in Christ and God's will for your life. If Satan can't keep you from believing in God, he'll try to deceive you into believing wrongly about God.

The same is true about giving. *It does matter where you give.* However, you would hardly know that by examining the giving of many Christians and churches. Every year millions and millions of dollars are contributed by Christians to organizations that oppose rather than support the cause of Christ. If all believers would become as knowledgeable in their giving as they are in their stock market investments, the resources of the body of Christ would be multiplied several times over.

Well, where should a Christian give his tithes and offerings?

Let's go back to our theme verse in the Fixed Law of Giving, Malachi 3:10, "Bring ye all the tithes [and offerings] into the storehouse, that these may be meat in mine house, and prove me now herewith, saith the Lord of hosts, if I will not open the windows of heaven, and pour out a blessing, that there shall not be room enough to receive it."

Where is God's storehouse? Is it not where you corporately gather to worship and feed on God's Word—your local church? I believe one of the main reasons why God has so blessed the PTL ministry is because we have always encouraged PTL viewers to join a local Bible-believing church and support it with their tithe.

Personally, I've been a member of a church all my life, and I support the church. I believe the church is the most important institution on earth today.

We have a close relationship with more than four thousand churches around the country who follow up the people who come to Christ through our ministry. I've had pastors tell me that more than half the people in their church have come through PTL referrals.

Still, sometimes media ministries are accused of draining money from local churches. A recent independent Gallup survey has proved just the opposite. The survey revealed that supporters of TV ministries tended to also be the top givers in their local churches. Not only that, but they tended to be the most prosperous people in the church. What a testimony to the rewards of giving!

Pastor John Gimenez of the great Rock Church in Virginia Beach, Virginia taught me a great lesson in checking our motives as to whether we are building our church or the Lord's church, our kingdom or the Lord's kingdom. He said, "Jim, whenever we go to build a building, we plant [give] seed in another church and try to pick one as close to ours as possible."

That's the real test in our giving motives. If we give to a church across the country, their gain is not going to threaten to draw our people away. However, if we give to bless our neighboring church so they will grow even with some of our members or potential members, that is "kingdom living." We need more of that.

So when we began to build our Partner Center, we did just that. We planted a $100,000 seed in a church just six miles down the highway from Heritage USA. That church is now growing and being blessed and the whole Christian community here is now blessed because we are working together rather than working in competition with one another.

If it had not been for the support of other ministries, our ministry could have never survived and accomplished what it has. In one of our most difficult times while trying to complete our church facility, Oral Roberts came and brought a hundred thousand dollars, and Rex Humbard came and brought fifty thousand dollars. Those gifts enabled us to move into the church debt-free just as we had believed God.

Then there were times when we had money in our tithe account where we have been able to give to those same ministries and others in their critical hour. I believe the main reason the body of Christ suffers lack today is because there is not that kind of cooperation and sharing among all ministries and churches.

God always provides enough for the whole family. Remember when God miraculously provided manna (bread) for the children of Israel in their wilderness journey (see Exodus 16)? God let the manna rain down from heaven in a big pile and the people could go out and gather it. It must have been miracle food because the Bible records that he that gathered much had nothing left over and he that gathered little had no lack (Ex. 16:18).

The body of Christ will be able to take care of itself and have sufficiency for all it needs if we will be obedient in our giving *individually* and *corporately*. The Apostle Paul expressed this to the Corinthians when he admonished them, "Right now you have plenty and can help them: then at some other time they can share with you when you need it. In this way each will have as much as he need" (II Cor. 8:14).

Perhaps, now you can understand why you need to support your *local church* with your tithe. But what about support for *ministries* like PTL?

The prophet declares that the Israelites were robbing God by withholding both tithes and "offerings." Offerings are gifts beyond the tithe which are given to support the work of God beyond the local church, across the nation and around the world. Without these offerings, ministries like ours could never exist. Why must they exist and be supported? Although there are many reasons, let me suggest just three:

1. *Evangelism*

Today, TV media ministries are reaching people for Christ that cannot be reached any other way.

Even door-to-door witnessing can't penetrate many of the modern security apartment/condominium complexes. Yet our TV broadcast reaches right into the living rooms, hospitals, prisons, etc., where people are. Every year we give to our followup pastors the names of thousands of new Christian contacts.

Over the past ten years, PTL has been helping to spark a worldwide revival, such as has not happened in centuries of missionary efforts. In Latin America, our Spanish PTL TV program has been rated the number one program in several countries. Our African PTL broadcast has had such an impact that national leaders seek out our host for counsel. In Japan, our viewership and response to the Gospel has doubled every year. In Italy, Thailand, and in Taiwan, our programs have broken down religious barriers and opened the hearts to the message of Christ.

Nowhere internationally are we trying to build our own kingdom. In every country, we try to use national hosts and support their work until they can establish support on their own. Then we turn the ministry over to them so we can then reach out to new countries.

2. *Information and Mobilization*

Have you noticed how the devil's crowd has come together lately? They've come out of their closets of sin and mobilized to get their way, in our government, schools, and media. If the body of Christ does not come together in a similar way, we can be defeated. Our Lord Jesus' high priestly prayer was that all his followers, the church, would come together in love. Only then would the world see that we are truly His (John 13:35).

PTL and other TV ministries are significant instruments of God to bring about that unity, both in word and deed. Every day at Heritage USA thousands of believers from every Christian denomination come to worship and learn together. Guests on our TV program, representing all parts of the body of Christ, draw people together with emphasis on Christ and His Word rather than divisive doctrine.

The Lord has used our broadcast to get believers to work together to meet needs of food, clothing, and medical supplies for the starving and refugees of Cambodia, Central America, India, and Africa; for flood victims in Virginia, West Virginia, Pennsylvania, Louisiana, and Arizona; and tornado victims in Mississippi and here in the Carolinas. None of these needs could have been met by a single church alone; but by mobilizing help from the body of Christ around the country, victory was won.

3. *Christian Awareness and Conscience*

I am intensely aware of the awesome opportunity and responsibility I have in being able to address millions of viewers on a daily basis.

There are issues that Christians must be aware of and responsibilities that they should be fulfilling.

For decades, the church has largely neglected its responsibility to care for the poor. As a result, we have the unworkable monstrosity of the government welfare system. At President Reagan's urging, we challenged our viewers and cooperating pastors to start Love Centers to care for the poor. Over 820 Centers across the country help millions of needy people.

Jesus said, "I was in prison and ye visited me." Our PTL Prison ministry has recruited and helped train more than 7,000 people to work in prison ministry.

For nearly ten years after the Wade vs. Rowe decision in 1973 to legalize abortion, much of the body of Christ was silent on this explosive issue. God convicted me that abortion was murder and I couldn't keep silent any longer. My verbal stand against abortion was costly, causing us to lose some of our most valuable TV affiliates and incurring wrath from government officials and others. But I had to do it to obey God. I believe this stand has helped many others to stand up as well. This and the starting of our home for women in crisis pregnancy as a positive alternative is helping to stem the tide of abortion in America no matter what the Supreme Court says.

On many, many other issues, like voting, pornography, child abuse, missions, and on and on, PTL has pricked the conscience of viewers and helped them to not just stand but to stand up for God and His ways, and work together for victory.

Our *attitude* in giving is probably as important as our *knowledge* in giving. I believe that if we give faith cheerfully to God, He will bless our tithes and offerings wherever we give. But like Paul, "I desire that fruit may abound to your account."

Our faithful PTL Partners will receive the credit and glory for all the souls won to Jesus by our ministry. That is the greatest and everlasting reward for our giving.

9

"Now Is the Time"
Testimonies

We have been talking about God's fixed law of giving. There is another fixed law of God that we need to discuss in conclusion. It is the law of timing. If you don't believe in the fixed law of timing, you'd better not be an astronaut. When they send your rocket to the moon, you'd better be in the right timing, otherwise you're going to miss the moon by a million miles.

Scientists call this timing "the window that opens." That's the period of time that you've got to shoot that rocket up and if you don't get it up at that time you'll miss the moon. To determine that window, scientists must study the timing and movement of the stars, earth, and moon.

We as God's people need to learn timing. If you're smart you learn there's a right time and a wrong time to ask the boss for a raise. You find out the right time to show up at your friend's fancy dinner party—not too early and not too late. The Bible says "there is a season and a time to every purpose under the heaven" (Eccl. 3:1).

In the fullness of time (or at the proper time) God

sent His Son to earth for us. At Gethsemane, Jesus said, "Now my time has come" (John 13:31) to be lifted up for our sins.

I'm convinced that now, the 1980's, is the time for the body of Christ. I don't think that there is a serious Bible scholar alive today that would argue that we are not living in the last days before the second coming of our Lord. Every biblical sign has been or is being fulfilled—the restoration of the nation of Israel, their gaining their capital of Jerusalem, the increase of wars and rumors of wars, the increase in knowledge, travel, earthquakes, signs in the heavens, false prophets and messiahs, spread of evil, and proclamation of the Gospel to the uttermost parts of the earth. All these prophecies of scriptures are being fulfilled before our very eyes.

The Bible tells us that Jesus, the Bridegroom, is not coming for a weak, emaciated, confused bride. No, He is coming for a glorious church, holy and without fault (Eph. 5:27). Jesus said, "I *will* build my church, and the gates of hell shall not prevail against it" (Matt. 16:18).

Now is the time that God is calling and preparing the Bride unto Himself. If ever there was a scripture for the church today, I believe it is Romans 13:11 which says, "Knowing the time, that *now* it is high time to awake out of sleep: for *now* is our salvation nearer than when we believed."

We know the time—it is *the* last days. The hour is upon us. What we are going to do, we must do *now*. Now is the time to stop sleeping, to stop talking about things, to stop waiting for things to happen to us. Now is the time to stand up; now is the time to take action; now is the time to invest in God's kingdom; now is the time to labor for the Master while there's still light.

In Matthew 24, Jesus clearly outlines the signs (which we've already listed) of His Second Coming. Then in the same setting in Matthew 25, He gives two important parables to urge His followers to be ready at His coming.

The first parable is about the five wise and five foolish virgins, going forth to meet the bridegroom. The wise virgins filled their lamps and were prepared though the bridegroom tarried. The foolish virgins let their lamps go out and slumbered until the bridegroom came. Then before they could get out to buy oil and come back, the door was closed and they were left out.

The second parable is the familiar story of the talents. The master left talents with his three servants: one received five, another two, and another, one. The one with five talents and the other with two each worked with their talents and doubled them for the master. The servant with one buried his. When the master returned, he rewarded the two faithful servants but cast the unprofitable servant out of his kingdom into outer darkness.

The point of these two parables is obvious. If we want to be ready when Christ returns, we had better be using our talents for the Lord, letting our light shine, and investing what we have for the Master's use.

At PTL, we have more than 2,000 employees, some of the greatest people in all the world. Do you know what I've found? The happiest people on our staff, the happiest people I know, are those that are 100% dedicated to God and His work and don't have to make excuses.

They are the *second* milers. They are not your typical 9 to 5 employee. They will always go the second mile. They will stay up all night to get the job done. They can see in faith the fruit of their labor and, therefore, there is joy in their work. This is the testimony of our Lord Jesus Christ—"who for the joy that was set before him endured the cross" (Heb. 12:2).

The only person happier than the second miler is a person who is married to a second miler. They share the labor and rewards together, so they too are second milers. Unfortunately, the reason that many a man or woman is not totally dedicated to God is because they have a husband or wife who won't let them be.

Instead of bellyaching all the time, that reluctant husband or wife would be much better off if he or she would make some hot soup and come down and stand by their mate and get involved in helping, too. When you begin to find a shared love, a working together in a team effort, you'll begin to find the greatest rewards man could ever know.

For not only will you find great fellowship with your mate and/or your co-worker but with the Lord. Do you know then when you do God's will, the Lord works with you? This is what the Bible says in Mark 16:20: "they went forth and preached everywhere, *the Lord working with them . . ."*

What a privilege it is to know as we labor for God's kingdom He is with us, helping strengthen us and recording our every gift, our every good deed for those eternal rewards. I know there are many of our Partners, many givers who have never made a mark on man's or society's hit parade. They've never got their name on any billboard or any "who's who" list. But they have made their mark on God's list.

They are people like Cornelius, of whom the Bible says "thy prayers and thine alms [giving] are come up for a memorial before God" (Acts 10:40). They are people like Dorcas, who "was full of good works and almsdeeds [giving to the needy] which she did" (Acts 9:36).

They are people like Bob and Jeanne Johnson of our PTL family. Bob and Jeanne are always there to help whenever I need them. And they are there before I can even ask for their help.

When we were building the Partner Center and were really struggling, Bob and Jeanne felt that they just had to help more than they were already doing. Despite the fact that they didn't have any money available, they gave $1,000 for a Lifetime Partnership by putting the amount on two credit cards.

Does God honor the second milers giving? Right after giving this gift, Bob and Jeanne received a large, totally unexpected gift. It was just enough for them to make the down payment on their dream house here at Heritage USA, something they'd been praying about for two years.

There are many more second milers in the following chapters of this book who like Bob and Jeanne have a good report to share with you. They are the faithful people of this world. And God honors faithfulness.

Do you know the hardest thing about giving? It is doing it. That may sound strange and oversimplified but it is true. *Getting anything started is half the battle*.

Faith without works is dead. I guarantee you that if these nine chapters have not motivated your faith to give, the following testimony chapters will. We have even divided the testimonies into different areas of blessing that you might focus on your needed harvest. Then all you have to do is to put your faith into action with obedience.

I hope in some way this book has challenged you. Some might even think I'm meddling, because for them, giving is a very personal subject. But I don't think there is anything wrong with being challenged.

Evangelist Mike Murdock says that the greatest thing I've ever done for him is to challenge his faith to give. Since I've encouraged him in this way, his giving has increased tenfold—but God's blessings back to him have increased a hundredfold. I'm believing that for you, too.

Begin to plant seed for a great harvest. Do it now. Now is the time for your blessing. God wills it. You can loose it and make it happen. Your life will never be the same!

Now that you understand these proven principles of giving, read the following actual testimonies of God faithfulness to pour out showers of blessings on those who give.

10

FINANCIAL BLESSINGS

JOINS VICTORY CLUB—RECEIVES $1000, JOINS LIFETIME—RECEIVES $10,000

I joined the Victory Club with money I had received to buy a new dress. In a couple of weeks my husband received a gift from a relative for $1000. Our bills were piling up, but my husband agreed to taking a Lifetime Partnership. We charged it on our Visa card. Within three weeks, we received a letter telling us that some land my husband had inherited years ago had sold for almost $10,000. I praise God for His faithfulness. He is a good God. Keep teaching on giving, it really works!

Patsy Watts
Wichita, Kansas

BORROWS FOR LIFETIME PARTNERSHIP—GETS TEN TIMES RETURN

I wanted to become a Lifetime Partner so much, but I didn't have the money. With my husband's okay, I borrowed the $1000 and joined and you know what? In a matter of days, that amount was multiplied back to us by ten times for our children's education. Praise the Lord!

Theresa Greenwood
Muncie, Indiana

79

JOINS VICTORY CLUB/RECEIVES CHECK FOR $1500

My husband isn't saved and he gets upset when I give to the Lord. But I felt so burdened for PTL that I sent a check for $25 for the Victory Club, and prayed that the Lord would help with the rest of the money. Three days later I received a check written out to me for $1500 on inherited land that had sold. I rejoined as I wrote a check for the rest of my Victory Club pledge. Giving to PTL has blessed me more than I can say.

Gayle Smith
Winter Springs, Florida

GIVES $1000 OUT OF NEED—BLESSED SIX TIMES OVER

I am forty-seven years old and have known God all my life, but I just found out what God can do when we give to Him. I gave $1000 out of my need to PTL. God gave it back to me six times over. I'm not a bit surprised about the big profit. You can't beat God in giving! Enclosed is a check for $300 to promote the Gospel.

Clifford H. Smith
Los Angeles, California

SENDS $100—FINDS MORE IN BANK ACCOUNT

After we sent $100 for the Girls' Home, the bank called and said we had $117 more than we thought in our account.

Robert Sell
Celina, Ohio

UNEXPECTED BUSINESS TRANSACTION

Back in April, I sent in $100 for the Victory Club. To be quite honest, I was very skeptical about all the testimonies of blessings that Partners were sending in about their giving. Well, now I believe! It took a couple of months. But exactly two months from the date of my gift, a business transaction occurred that brought in an unexpected $975 to me.

Diane Schleper
Aurora, Illinois

RECEIVES UNEXPECTED $11,598.52

When I mailed to you my $100 check to become a Lifetime Partner, I had to borrow the money—but I did so much wish to help build the PTL Partner Center.

Exactly two months later, I received an unexpected check in the mail for $11,598.52. God does repay ten times over!

All I want now is to come visit the PTL Partner Center with my daughter.

Edna Phelps
Edmonton, Alberta, Canada

JOINS VICTORY CLUB/RECEIVES FIVE TIMES AS MUCH

I pledged and sent my check for $100 for the Victory Club. Within a week, we received in the mail a check for almost five times that amount. Praise the Lord!

O.T.
Boise, Idaho

PLEDGE $100—RECEIVE $500

Through PTL, our faith is strengthened every day. On Tuesday, May 29th, I was watching PTL. You, Jim, preached that "Faith without works is dead" and Tammy sang "Now Is The Time". The entire program really spoke to my heart. I realized that Now Is The Time to join the Victory Club—not next month or after we got out of the financial bind we were in. Now Is The Time to step out in faith and plant that seed. My husband agreed. We phoned PTL right away and pledged $100 on our Visa card. That Friday, we received an unexpected check in the mail for $500. The Lord surely provides!

Mrs. Karen Nobles
Conesus, New York

FAITH PUT TO WORK—GETS RETURN ON GIVING

I always believed in giving to God's work and finally realized I had to put my faith to work. I mailed my first $25 for the Victory Club, but I knew I couldn't afford it.

That week, I sold fifty dollars worth of homemade crafts. Then, on my birthday, my employer gave me a good raise and eight more hours of work a week. Not only that, but my family also gave me $85 for my birthday. At one time, I thought I couldn't afford to give, but now I realize I can't afford *not* to. May God continue to bless you and PTL.

M.S.
Brunswick, Georgia

THANKS PTL FOR LETTING HER HELP SAVE BABIES

I wanted to send $100 to the Girls' Home, but I just didn't have the money. Then I got a profit-sharing check from a job I quit over two years ago. What a surprise. I'm glad this gift came in time to help you at PTL. Thank you for letting me help save the babies.

Mary Mosely
Wrightstown, Georgia

THEY GAVE—AND RECEIVED

My husband and I decided to join the Victory Club. Soon after we sent in our money, I received over $100. The following week, my husband received $800 from his grandmother's estate. Not only are we paying our bills, but we are helping people through PTL all over the world. Praise God! It feels mighty good to give and receive.

J.S.
Aulander, North Carolina

HEARTFELT WISH IS GRANTED

When you offered the Lifetime Partnership, I wanted to join so bad but I knew I couldn't come up with $1000. I sent my monthly pledge and the $25 extra for the Victory Club. The very next day, my mother called and said she was sending $1000 in my name for a Lifetime Partnership. I just praise the Lord for this, my heart's desire.

Robert Fowierk
Nappanee, Indiana

$300 RETURN ON VICTORY CLUB

I mailed in my first payment for the Victory Club and $25 for a First Aid Kit for Victory. Well, much to my surprise, a check came in the mail for $300. Here is the balance on my Victory Club pledge. Isn't God wonderful!

Peggy Vickery
Smyrna, Georgia

LOST CHECK FOR $1000 FOUND
AFTER PLEDGING $100

One night I pledged $100 by phone for the Victory Club. The next day, I found a check for $1000 that had been lost since December. Glory to God! He is so good!

J.R.
Harmony, Minnesota

LIFETIME PARTNER IN IOWA

I pledged $1000 for a Lifetime Partnership but didn't have the money or any foreseeable way of getting it. Praise God, I received just that amount from a totally unexpected source! Now I have a lifetime vacation place just from stepping out in faith.

Eugenia K. Todd
Mediapolis, Iowa

PLEDGED IN FAITH—GOD HONORED

We joined the Victory Club in faith because we didn't have the money. Now we do. In fact, since we pledged, my husband received a $200 rebate on a bill and I received $195 on a past due check.

J.P.
Pittsfield, Massachusetts

FINANCIAL BLESSING AND JOB PROVIDED

Last month, I sent you a check for $65 as partial payment for the Victory Club. And, boy, did we ever need victory. That was all the money we had! Since it wasn't enough to pay our rent or utilities anyway, I decided to send it as seed for a miracle. Praise God, it happened! In the mail, we got the money to pay our rent and utilities and also to send the rest for the Victory Club. Then, this week, my husband got called back to work on a job!

Jan Petty
Winter Beach, Florida

$500 CHECK AFTER JOINING VICTORY CLUB

I wanted to write and let you know that after I sent you my $100 check to join the Victory Club, a $500 check came in the mail. *I was anticipating nothing* in return for the offering. I just felt compelled to send this gift to PTL, and I was mightily surprised when that check arrived!

Mrs. Maureen McWatters
Birmingham, Michigan

IRS BLESSINGS

About two weeks ago, we made a sacrificial gift to PTL for the Victory Club. This was really hard to do and I wasn't sure we could really do that since I had to recently quit my job to care for our new baby. However, the very afternoon we sent our gift, we received a letter from the IRS stating that we had made a mistake on our tax return and were entitled to $200 more in our return. Then, yesterday, I received $250 in the mail from an unexpected source. Enclosed is 10% of that gift for more victory.

N.P.
Flemington, Pennsylvania

RECEIVED $3500 AFTER JOINING VICTORY CLUB

On May 17th, I took a step of faith by sending $25 for my first payment on the Victory Club. We desperately needed a financial miracle. Praise the Lord, on May 26th, my husband received $3500. God opened up the windows of heaven and poured out a blessing that we didn't have room enough to hold!

Lillian Moreland
Lake Lyn, Pennsylvania

TEN TIMES RETURN ON LIFETIME MEMBERSHIP

We had been receiving checks from an insurance policy that was due to end in March. Our first thought was "Go ahead, give $1000 to the Lord and see what happens". So in January, we sent our check for $1000 to join the Lifetime Partnership. Much to our surprise, we were informed in late February that these payments would continue for another year. We were blessed with nearly a ten-fold return on our seed gift.

Dale & Lucille Mock
Grand Island, New York

RECEIVES BONUS OF $5000 BEFORE MAILING $100 GIFT

I had a burden to send in money to PTL for a week. I made out a check for $100 but didn't get it in the mail because I needed the Zip code. I thought God wouldn't bless me because I failed to get the check mailed that day. Well, I was wrong. That night my husband came home from work and told me he is getting a $5000 bonus! Praise God for His wonderful blessing. Keep up the great work you are doing at PTL!

J.J.
Wharton, Texas

VICTORY CLUB—LAW OF MULTIPLICATION

I thank God every day for PTL and The Inspirational Network. I joined the PTL Partner family and have not missed a month in sending my $25 pledge.

I recently sent $125 for the Victory Club. I am retired and live on a fixed income, so I had a very hard time stretching my money from month to month.

I don't know how, but since I have been giving, my checking account stays $500–800 ahead all the time!

I consider it an honor and a privilege to help support your ministry for what it is doing for the glory of God!

Wilma Stertz
Milford, Ohio

GIFT WAS RETURNED—DOUBLED

I gave $10 to Jim and Tammy to put toward the fabulous Girls' Home, and although it was not a great sum, I got it back doubled. There really is victory in Jesus!

Lisa Milloway
Greensboro, North Carolina

FIRST AID KIT—SENT FOR
AND RECEIVED $150

I was watching your show this morning and decided to send my $25 for the First Aid Kit. At the time I only had $40 to my name. While I was writing this letter to PTL, the mailman came with Federal and State tax checks for $150. Praise God!

G.G.
Long Beach, California

SENT $100, RECEIVED $1200

I sent $100 for the Victory Club. The very next day, I received $1200. I'm joining in intercessory prayer for PTL for a great victory now!

Anna Guze
Trenton, New Jersey

JOINS VICTORY CLUB—GETS TWO CHECKS TOTALING $650

Last September, I fell down some stairs at work and hurt my back and hip. Funds were kind of low since then, but in April I joined the Victory Club and things changed. God had blessed me with a check for $390 and another check for $260. It couldn't have come at a better time. Praise the Lord!

M.B.
Modesto, California

VICTORY CLUB—IMMEDIATE RETURN

We have a small bank account for a five member family, but I wanted to send $100 and join the Victory Club. My husband told me to send it, but not to expect anything back. I said, "God will bless us some way". Several days later, we were given $100. God is so faithful!

Pam McCarty
Willow Grove, Pennsylvania

FROM MONTHLY PARTNER—TO VICTORY CLUB—TO LIFETIME PARTNER

My husband and I have seen such a wonderful change in our lives since we became involved in the PTL ministry. We became PTL Partners even though we were stretched to the breaking point financially. We couldn't afford it, but we started giving more to PTL and to our church. Praise God, everything worked out fine! We received a surprise financial gift and were able to pay off everything we owed. Since then, we joined the Victory Club and became PTL Lifetime Partners. God really blesses His children.

Mr. & Mrs. Walter E. Mackey III
Newport News, Virginia

DOUBTS ALLAYED

I watch and enjoy your program regularly and often wished to be able to send $1000 or $100. But because of being on a strict budget and supporting my home church, I didn't feel I could. Then Jesus impressed me to write a $25 check to you.

Well, I wrote out the check but argued with God, "You are going to have to supply this back because I don't have $25 to send."

Then I said, "If you do this before the end of the month, I'll know it's you and not just my thoughts."

I wasn't thinking that it was May 29th, which only left 2 days. On Thursday, the 31st, I received $49.56 that I forgot was due me. Through this, God is lifting my faith.

N.A.
York, Pennsylvania

LIFETIME PARTNERSHIP DOUBLES BLESSINGS

I gave $1000 to become a Lifetime Partner, and to my surprise, $2000 mysteriously appeared in my bank account. The bank told me that yes, the money was definitely mine. An insurance company had deposited in my account the balance they had owed me for several years.

I then sent another $1000 to become a Lifetime Partner again. My husband just recently passed away, and after going through some old papers, I found a $20,000 life insurance policy in his name that I didn't even know existed.

I praise God for His miracle blessings!

Ruth Kleinknecht
Bridgeport, Connecticut

SINCE GIVING, THEY ARE RECEIVING

Since my husband and I have been giving to God's work, wonderful things have happened. We sent in $100 for the PTL Bible and the next week received a $2000 inheritance from an uncle I hadn't seen in years. We planted another seed by sending in $125 to the Victory Club. We were expecting $200 in our tax return, but the check came with a letter saying our taxman had made a mistake. Instead, the check was for $690. Praise the Lord!

Mrs. Wayne Johnson
Three Rivers, Michigan

UNEXPECTED TAX REFUND AFTER JOINING VICTORY CLUB

I pledged $100 to join the Victory Club. The mail arrived with a totally unexpected tax refund check for $100.

Mirabell Hanna
Williamstown, West Virginia

FIRST AID VICTORY KIT REPORT

My husband and I decided to order the "First Aid

Kit To Victory" as "seed for our need". I had major surgery five years ago and we had lots of medical bills.

The same day we were to mail the check, there was an envelope in the mail from our local bank. Enclosed was a check for $500 with a note saying the giver wished to remain anonymous.

Praise the Lord! He gave it back running over before we even mailed our check!

Don & Dianna Fowler
Union, Missouri

GETTING OUT OF DEBT BY GIVING TO LIFETIME MEMBERSHIP

We have always had our own business. It was prosperous but somehow we had $250,000 stolen from us.

After a few months, we were still $190,000 in debt. Nevertheless, both my husband and I felt led to become Lifetime Partners. We sent in our $1000 and a $15 monthly pledge.

A few days later, two of the companies we owed debts to called us. We owed one company $2800, and the other one $2750. Both companies said they would take $1000 each and mark us paid in full. Right there, God blessed us with $3550.

My husband is claiming that God will bless us so abundantly that we will be completely clear of debt. God bless you richly!

Arthur and Geraldine Fore
Ceres, California

TAX BENEFIT

For months, I wrestled with the idea of becoming a Lifetime Partner, believing I should join but not having the money.

Then I thought the Memberships were closed. When you opened up the memberships again, I had to be obedient to God and join!

The next week, we filed our income tax and were told that the government owed us $1700 over a period of 4 years back. Isn't that like God, when we are obedient.

J.H.
Atlanta, Georgia

JOINING VICTORY CLUB AGAIN

My husband and I joined the Victory Club, and our David and Goliath arrived in the mail, along with a check for $275. The next day, we got another check for $240. We mailed the balance of $50 on our Victory Club the following morning, and that same afternoon, I received $90 in the mail. Praise the Lord! Enclosed is $100 for our second Victory Club membership.

Bill & Jane Ford
Portland, Oregon

GIVES TO NEED—GETS OWN NEED MET

We live entirely on Social Security, and $100 is a lot of money to us. However, my husband was touched by your financial need and joined the Victory Club. Much to his surprise, a wholly unexpected check for $1000 came in the mail. Praise the

Lord for His goodness! We love God and the PTL Family.

Mrs. Gaylord Dubois
Orange City, Florida

COURT LITIGATION SETTLES AFTER GIVING

Last week, I wrote and pledged $100 for the Victory Club, not knowing where the money would come from. Our phone had been disconnected, things were so bad. Well, two days later, my husband came home and told me a court litigation which has been going on for two years was settled. We would be receiving five thousand greatly needed dollars.

We always stand with you on Matthew 18:19. Your program has literally saved my life twice!

P.D.
Arlington, Indiana

WIDOW GIVES $1000 IN FAITH—RECEIVES 24 TIMES ON INSURANCE POLICY

My husband died in March of this year and I thought he had dropped his life insurance. I decided to look into it anyway. In the meantime, I sent $1000 on my American Express Card for a Lifetime Membership. In July, I received a check from the insurance company for $24,322.19. Praise God! I know He is alive!

Ruth Curry
Memphis, Tennessee

LIFETIME PARTNERSHIP—$3000 AND A JOB PROMOTION

We gave $1000 to become Lifetime Partners, even though it left us with about $400. Within three or four weeks, God gave it back to us threefold. Not only did God give us $3000, but my husband, who worked as a car salesman on straight commission, got a promotion making over $30,000 per year. Now we can give more to PTL.

Gene & Becky Cowart
Phenix City, Alabama

AN UNEXPECTED CLAIM SETTLEMENT

When you offered the Lifetime Partnerships, I wanted so badly to join but when I checked my credit card accounts, they were both to the limit!

Mother came to my rescue and loaned me the money to join. After I sent the check, we got a call from an attorney offering to settle a seven-year claim for $7500. We hadn't expected anything from it. It is enough to pay off all our debts and the loan, too. The Lord has done so much for me and my family.

W.R.
N. Huntingdon, Pennsylvania

$50 SEED HARVESTS $2000

When I sent you fifty dollars a couple of weeks ago, I just knew that God would do a miracle. He did! I just received two checks, for a total of two thousand dollars.

Deborah Clendenin
Port St. Lucie, Florida

VICTORY CLUB—UNEXPECTED BONUS

I sent my first $25 to join the Victory Club and about two weeks later my husband received a $500 bonus. Here is our second $25. We can't wait to see what the Lord has in store for us this time.

Jim & Kay Chadwick
Hayes, Virginia

FORTY-FIVEFOLD RETURN IN ONE WEEK

Last week, we sent in for the David and Goliath statue, asking God for victory in our finances. In so doing, not only were our prayers answered, but our $100 gift was multiplied to almost $4500.

Bruce & Brend Carlson
Boynton Beach, Florida

RECEIVE BONUS BEFORE MAILING CHECK FOR VICTORY CLUB

I wrote out a check for the Victory Club, placed it on my dresser, and waited to tell my husband. We are trying to accumulate extra money to buy a house with and I knew the $100 would need an explanation. My husband came home and before I even had a chance to tell him, he handed me a bonus check from work for $2500. The storehouses of heaven were opened for us!

Paula Bund
Holbrook, New York

SOCIAL SECURITY CHECKS LOOSED

My Social Security checks had been held up for a long time. So I sent in $25 for the Victory Club with a prayer that God would provide these.

Only 4 hours later I received in the mail my six Social Security checks, totalling $1700.

R.H.
Arlington, Virginia

TAX MIRACLE

We owed the IRS $22,000 in back taxes, and it was due immediately. We sent in our last $100 to PTL to support the People That Love Home.

The next week, my husband got a raise at work, so we were able to go to the bank and take out a second mortgage on our house to totally pay off the IRS. My husband's raise covers the mortgage payments.

Judy Brittingham
Dunwoody, Georgia

CHRISTMAS SAVINGS RETURNED FORTY-FOLD

I'd been having real financial difficulty this year. In October, I saw one of your ministry programs on giving and receiving. I asked myself, "Where can I get money to give?" and I thought of my Christmas savings of just over a hundred dollars.

In faith, I sent it to PTL, asking God to somehow return it by Christmas. On December 9th, I was called at work by a lawyer saying he had a $4000 check for me. I couldn't believe he was talking to the right person. It was coming from a car accident over 3 years ago. I had told the lawyer not to pursue the case, but God had other ideas.

Paula Taltocco
Schenectady, New York

GOD BLESSED THEIR STAND OF FAITH
Since taking a stand of faith to send PTL $10 each month, our finances have changed from not being able to pay half of our bills (75% medical) to where we're paying all the bills and having money left over. We appreciate your standing with us for this miracle.

Susan Dudley
Whitehouse, Texas

TAMMY HELPED ME GIVE
Tammy really helped us begin to give by what she shared on your program. It so convicted us that my husband and I wrote out a check for $50, all the money we had for the month, and sent it to you. The next day, a close friend brought me an envelope. It contained $50, which she said she was led to give us. Now I've learned the friend has been unexpectedly blessed with a gift worth $100.

Redge & Jan Peifer
Mt. Clemens, Michigan

BLESSINGS AND BLESSINGS
Your program brought me to Jesus so recently I sent a check for $100 to join the Victory Club and get the PTL Parallel Bible.

The day my Bible arrived, I received a letter and

check from a company I'd worked for years ago, sending $310 profit I earned five years back.

The next day, I received a call from a person who had bumped my old car in the back. He was insisting I take $200 for the accident.

A week later, my health insurance company sent me a $407 refund and the bank corrected a $125 checkbook error in my favor. A total blessing of $1042!

> *D. L.*
> *Bricktown, New Jersey*

A QUICK RETURN

Two days after we sent in $25 asking for the Don't Give Up Album (money we didn't have to spare but God told me to send it anyway), we received an unexpected check for $86. Praise the Lord!

> *H.H.*
> *Muscatine, Iowa*

STUDENT GRANT PROVIDED

In faith, I sent a check to PTL for $50. Exactly four days later, I received a letter with a check and grant for $10,500 from the university I hoped to attend.

> *Mark Carlson*
> *Madison, Wisconsin*

A SOLID GOLD VICTORY WINNER!

I've been watching your show for about 3 months now, and I found myself moved to pledge $20 a month. I didn't even tell my husband right away because money is a bit tight for us and we've only been married a year and a half.

Well, I'm a contest nut—I never win big, but I always enter everything. I heard about a contest on a station here in Los Angeles, in which they were giving away gold coins. So, I prayed, "Hey, God, I would really love to win that gold. I'm not sure if you think I should win or not, but if you would let me win so I could catch up on our bills, I promise not to be stingy—I'll share it with you by sending one of the coins to PTL." In the meantime, I kept watching your show and something just kept telling me to join the Victory Club. So I went to the bank and made out a $50 cashier's check. Before I could even mail that first Victory Club payment, they called my name on the radio! The station called me to say that I had indeed been the winner—12 gold coins worth $1,272! I hope it's okay that I send you a $100 check instead of a ¼ ounce gold coin. Thanks for all your good shows!

Beth Andrews
N. Hollywood, California

JOINS VICTORY CLUB—HUSBAND GETS RAISE
A couple of days after I joined the Victory Club my husband got a $300 a month raise. Praise God! Thank you so much for being faithful in ministering to us on TV. I do daycare for preschoolers and don't get a chance to be with other women. I truly need your program, so praise God for PTL!

Mrs. Ruth Arnold
Elk Grove, California

BLESSINGS ARE STILL COMING

This fall, I pledged and gave PTL $100 for the beautiful Bible and $15 in a monthly pledge. Already, God has turned that $100 in $1500 in blessings and that $15 pledge into $800. His blessings still haven't stopped coming.

J.S.
Porterville, California

NOW A BELIEVER—IT HAPPENED TO HIM

I must tell you that I honestly wondered if all the people that you told about receiving such blessing after giving were really true. Now I know beyond a shadow of doubt, because it happened to me.

Less than two weeks after I sent my pledge, my husband received a sum of money from a source we could of never dreamed of—his retirement was being raised!

V.D.
Houston, Texas

BLESSED EVEN BEFORE GIVING

We pledged to become Lifetime Partners. Even before we could scrape together the money to put it in the mail, I received an unexpected check in the mail for $6000 in Workman's Compensation.

R.L.
Far Rockaway, New York

RENT REDUCED

For months, I have been convicted to support your ministry but as a working single parent, I just couldn't see how I could fit it in to our already tight budget.

Finally in faith, I gave a one-time gift on my American Express card and pledged to become a monthly partner. First I got a bonus at work that more than covered the one-time gift. Then I received notice from the owners of my apartment that they were reducing my rent $50 a month, more than three times the monthly pledge I'd made.

G.W.
Kilgore, Texas

SEED FAITH SPROUTED

Several weeks ago, Oral Roberts was on your program asking that everyone plant a seed of faith. We sent $25. A few weeks later, we received notice that our property taxes were reduced $200 annually. Praise the Lord! That was unexpected!

D.J.
Homedale, Idaho

IT KEEPS INCREASING

Since becoming Lifetime Partners with you, our financial situation has for strange reasons changed. Our church giving has increased; our giving to PTL has increased, and yet our bank balance has also increased.

Most of all, our family's spiritual life and unity have also increased.

C.G.
Louisville, Kentucky

TWICE-BLESSED

When I first sent you $1000 to become Lifetime Partners, the Lord sent us an unexpected check for $10,000.

So we joined the Lifetime Partnership again with $1000. This time the Lord blessed me back with $1114.06 and has just made my husband part owner in the company where he is working. My husband's boss is putting him in his will and opening the company stock for my husband to purchase.

> *J.H.*
> *Atlanta, Georgia*

MARRIAGE SAVED AND FINANCIAL BLESSING

I'd been watching your program for three months since I'd been out of work. My bank balance had gotten down to $5.76, so out of my need, I called and pledged to become a monthly partner.

Two days later, I received a check for $139.60.

Your program is the reason my husband and I are still together and are going to make it.

> *V.C.*
> *Washington, D.C.*

IT DOES WORK

I have to tell you that once I gave my pledge last week, on Saturday, a very good friend of mine gave me $200. The Lord is truthful and it does work—when you give, you'll get your gift returned in full and overflowing measure, pressed down, shaken together, and running over (Luke 6:38).

> *M.R.*
> *Tampa, Florida*

UNEXPECTED $50 GIFT

The same day I mailed $25.00 for the Victory Club I received $50.00 I was not expecting. The Lord is blessing me in my home to witness for Jesus. I am 78 years old.

M.D.
Jacksonville, Arkansas

TWICE AS BLESSED

By faith, I sent $100 to join the Victory Club. I knew I didn't have it to give. But I've been watching how you have given and God has blessed you so I decided to trust God for it, too.

God not only blessed me back with the $100, he gave me $200 so I could get a phone installed in my home. I use it to witness for the Lord.

R.M.
Hemphill, West Virginia

SWEEPSTAKES WINNER

About the start of the year, the Lord convicted me to start tithing to the church and I have. Then I felt led also to become a Lifetime Partners. A few weeks after I did that, I discovered I'd won a trip for four to Disneyland, all expenses paid, worth over $2000. My husband was wanting to fly somewhere on vacation, so this is really a blessing. I know the Lord has His hand even on the sweepstakes.

B.A.
Dallas, Texas

FREE TRAVEL

While we were at PTL, we joined both the Lifetime Partnership and the Victory Club, and the blessings started to flow! We got to the airport for our trip home, and the airline had overbooked the flight. They asked for volunteers to be bumped from the flight, and since we had all our bases covered at home, we decided to wait.

Well, the wait turned out to be only 47 minutes, and we flew home first-class on an airline, with two vouchers in our pockets to fly anywhere the airline flies, round-trip, good for one year.

Needless to say, we intend to use them to return to PTL!

K.A.
Richmond, Michigan

11

HOUSING MIRACLES

HUNDREDFOLD RETURN ON HOUSE SALE
We gave $1000 to PTL to become Lifetime Partners. The very next day, a realtor here in Oregon called and offered $120,000 cash for a building we had for sale for a long time. That's over 100 times the amount of our $1000 one-time gift! I knew it was a direct answer to prayer. This is one of God's fixed laws of giving and receiving. We received over a hundredfold return on our gift. Everyone should invest in God's kingdom.

> Bruce Binkemeier
> Lake Oswego, Oregon

RECEIVED HOME
My Victory Club prayer request is already answered. Yesterday, we had written you to pray for a home for my husband and me. When my husband came home last night, he said our prayers are answered. We sign papers today.

> F.B.
> Grand Bay, Alabama

PROPERTY SELLS
We became Lifetime Partners a couple of months

ago. The closing of our property is this week, giving us a profit of over $13,000.

Even more important has been the inner healing in our lives since you brought us from the brink of disaster to the brink of a miracle.

T.D.
Schenectady, New York

PROVES GOD—RECEIVES BLESSING
In February of this year, I put my mobile home up for sale so I could move near my family. I was holding my monthly pledge for two months to have money to move with. I found an apartment to move into but there were no prospects for the sale of my home.

While in prayer one day, the Lord said to prove home and He would open up the windows of heaven. The next day I mailed in that money to PTL. On the following day, I got a buyer for my mobile home. Three days after I moved I got an additional $315.

Also, I had been wanting to join the Lifetime Partnerships, so I sent in my $100 and pledged the rest. In just a few weeks, I received an unexpected check for $1,996.90 and paid off the balance on my pledge. Isn't God wonderful!

M.G.
Columbus, Ohio

HOME SOLD AFTER THREE YEARS
I would like to join the Victory Club again! I have joined once already and started seeing victory and know that God is working in my life.

We have been trying to sell our home for three years. Two days after I mailed my $100, I got a call from a realtor saying the people who wanted to buy our home had been approved and we could close that week.

I know it was because of God! PRAISE THE LORD!

L.H.
Plant City, Florida

BLESSINGS AND BLESSINGS

It seems that since we've been giving to God, He's been blessing us, and blessing us, and blessing us.

Last month, the Lord told us to give PTL $1,000, and we did. About two weeks later, we sold a lot worth $30, to us. Praise the Lord—what a blessed God He is!

Since then, we have sold some apartments for $740,000 and have a contract on a special home we built for $195,000.

Thank you God! In Jesus' name.

Craig & Pam Hudson
Nassau, Delaware

LAND SALE/JOB RAISE

The very next day after we sent in our $100 pledge for the Heritage House and $1000 for our Lifetime Partnership, I received a $9000 a year raise at work.

The very same week, we were able to sell some land we wanted to release.

E.C.
Campti, Louisiana

MOBILE HOME SOLD AFTER JOINING VICTORY CLUB

My husband and I were praying for the sale of our mobile home in Oregon for the last two and a half years. We had buyers three different times, but each one fell through. Then we joined the Victory Club and within one week the Lord sent us a firm buyer and the mobile home was sold. We praise God for His mercy and grace upon His people!

Bob & Joyce Johnson
Chicago, Illinois

QUITE A PROFIT

This spring, the Lord led us to become Lifetime Partners twice, once for us and once for our little girls.

About that time, we needed to move south because of my husband's work. God sold our house in two days for a profit of $80,000. Now He's given us a beautiful country home in our new location. Jesus is so wonderful!

M.R.
Rock Hill, South Carolina

GAVE $1000—GOT HOME SHE PRAYED FOR

On May 24th, I sent in $1000 for a Lifetime Partnership. At the time I needed and was praying for a home in the Dallas area. I called PTL to pray with me. That very night I got a call to see a home the next day. This home has all the things I needed. It is in the area near churches, schools, jobs and shopping. It includes all appliances, $300 worth of plants, and there is even a $5000 discount. Thank God and bless PTL.

Dora Jordan
Longview, Texas

HOUSE SELLS AFTER TAKING LIFETIME PARTNERSHIP

I had been trying to sell my house. I sent $1000 for a Lifetime Partnership and $100 for the Girls' Home. Before I could even get to the Post Office, the house was sold!

Lena & Robert Kelley
Brenton, Alabama

BECAME LIFETIME PARTNER—HOUSE SELLS FOR $3500 MORE

I sent my $1000 for a Lifetime Partnership. At the same time, I put my house up for sale. The buyers did not negotiate a price, they raised it $3500.

C.K.
Bradenton, Florida

GIVES $1000—GAINS IN HEALING AND FINANCE

We had a condominium up for sale for a year and could not sell it. Also, my husband had a massive stroke and heart attack. We decided to pledge $1000 for a Lifetime Partnership and were led to send the money right away as seed faith. Our apartment sold the next day after sending the check. Also, my husband is regaining his health.

He has strength in his leg and his heart is now normal in size.

PRAISE THE LORD!

Mrs. Nils K. Olsen
Pompano Beach, Florida

BUILDING TOGETHER

This is a testimony of appreciation. Last winter we began to build our "dream house". At the same time, you were building the Partner Center and we were led to become Lifetime Partners. Our thought was, Together We Build.

We took the $1000 out of our construction account, not knowing for sure how we'd finish without it. But then my husband got a $1500 bonus check more than covering our gift. How wonderful the Lord is! Our Lifetime Membership card arrived the very same day we moved into our new house.

B.B.
Poquoson, Virginia

GIVES $1000 OUT OF NEED—THIRTY-TWO TIMES RETURN

I joined the Victory Club and wanted to become a Lifetime Partner but I really could not afford it. I prayed that God would make a way and send the $1000 out of my need. Several days later I sold two acres of land for $32,000. God certainly does make a way!

Jan Parson
Nokesville, Virginia

HOUSE SELLS AFTER JOINING THE VICTORY CLUB

My mother's house was up for sale for three and a half years. Within a month after joining the Victory Club, the house sold. PRAISE GOD FOR ANSWERED PRAYER.

> R.P.
> S. Wayne, Indiana

SELLS AIRPLANE AFTER BECOMING LIFETIME PARTNER

My husband and his partner had been trying to sell their airplane for months. I took a step of faith and joined the Lifetime Partnership and prayed with one of the PTL prayer counselors. My husband sold the plane the very next day. Jesus is so good and truly gives us the desires of our heart. Enclosed is a $100 Victory Club gift for the unwed mothers' home. God bless you all!

> Teresa Reed
> Metairie, Louisiana

SURPRISE BLESSING

Thank you for giving us the opportunity to become Lifetime Partners. We never expected any special blessings from joining. Then suddenly, the building we are living in went to co-op. We are now in the process of legally selling our "Tenant's Rights" to the apartment for $15,000. That makes a nice down-payment for a home we've wanted for so long.

> A.A.
> New York, New York

HOME SELLS FOUR DAYS AFTER SENDING PRAYER REQUEST

We mailed a prayer request on May 27th to PTL for our house to be sold. The house was listed on the market on May 29th. The Lord sent us a buyer on May 31st. Also, my son got a job two days after we sent in the request. PRAISE HIM!

Mrs. Lois Striedl
Toledo, Ohio

A MIRACLE HOUSE

Praise the Lord I joined PTL as a Lifetime Partner.

My husband and I had saved some money for a down payment on a house, but I knew God was telling me to send $1000 of it to PTL. I was so afraid we would need it.

Almost a week after I sent it, I called about a house we saw a few times—it didn't look very special from the road. But I found out it has 9.6 acres of land, 3 bedrooms, and 1088 square feet!

I called PTL and a wonderful lady there prayed and agreed with me that we would get the house, and nothing would come against us getting the loan.

The next day, the lady said she would let us have the house "as-is", with all appliances, air conditioner, washer, dryer, the largest freezer I've ever seen, a house full of furniture, and a dishwasher. Praise the Lord! All for $20,000!

Tammy always says, "You can get more interest on your money giving to the Lord's work than putting it in the bank." I'm one more happy person convinced of that!

E.W.
Pinson, Texas

A DOUBLE VICTORY MIRACLE

My house had been up for sale for a year and I called PTL for prayer concerning the sale.

While taking out the trash, a man stopped and asked if any houses on the street were for sale. He loved my house and bought it!

The Lord told me to send PTL $100, so I sent it, and soon thereafter, I received four checks totalling $154.40. Praise God!

Gladys Everhard
Venice, Florida

THANKS TO YOU AND THE LORD

We became double Lifetime Partners during the time of your building the Partner Center. At the time, we had no plans to sell our home though we had tried unsuccessfully to sell it the summer before.

However, this spring we saw a new home we liked. We listed our home, it sold in two months; the contractor accepted $7000 less for the new home and added extras; even the timing of the sale and new home was perfect.

We feel this has happened thanks to you and the Lord.

M.F.
Dallastown, Pennsylvania

115

LAND SOLD WITHOUT TRYING

Last month, we sent you a check for $60. It wasn't easy out of our farm budget, but we gave out of our need.

That evening, we received an offer on part of our land that we rarely use. The land is only good for hunting and trees. The offer was $600 an acre for 60 acres, a total of $36,000 from a seed offering of $60. We hadn't even put the land up for sale.

D.P.
Brooklyn, Michigan

GRANT TOWARD THE RENT

During your recent telethon, I became a monthly partner even though I'm on a small fixed income and it had been very hard for me to pay my current monthly bills.

Now wonderful things have opened up for me. HUD has granted me a sizeable amount towards my rent which will give me enough to pay bills and something extra.

P.S.
Waverly, New York

12

CARS

GETS CAR AFTER BECOMING MONTHLY PARTNER

My husband and I needed a car badly but really couldn't afford the one we wanted. Nevertheless, I felt that we should join PTL as $15 monthly partners as a show of faith. Praise God, in two weeks, we had that car!

John & Joni Blystone
Norwalk, Ohio

VICTORY CLUB—SENDS $10—GETS TEN TIMES RETURN

Not too long ago, I sent in $100 on the Victory Club. Ten days later, I received 10 times that amount back by selling a car we had been trying to sell for about 2 months. Thank God for His blessings!

Joan Cundiff
Louisville, Kentucky

SOLD TWO VEHICLES

I never heard of seed planting until I saw your program. Now I know it works! Last Friday, we sent $2000 to join as double Lifetime Partners.

Since that time, we have sold two vehicles that we couldn't sell for months. We got our exact price, more than what we paid for our Partnerships.

D.S.
Little Rock, Arkansas

BRAND NEW MUSTANG

Two months ago, you invited me to send in my prayer requests and I did. A week later, I decided to become a monthly partner with you and that very week, I received a brand new Ford Mustang. It was the car I'd wanted for over two years. God has answered my four other requests. Praise God, He loves us so much!

Wanda Moffett
Clovis, California

NEW CAR AND REFUND

Our bills have been equal to or more than what we have been making, but my husband gave me permission for us to join as monthly partners.

Last month was our first month to send support. We had just gotten a car and it was totalled in an accident. Not only did we get a new car, we got a $68 refund we didn't expect.

P.G.
Topeka, Kansas

SOLD AFTER A YEAR OF TRYING

Since I began as a Partner, God is working miracles in my life. My husband is not yet a Christian, so it's been hard to give. I really wanted to give for the

Victory Club, but was afraid to ask. When I did, my husband surprised me by saying it could be for my birthday. Praise God, just two days later, we sold a car we weren't using and had been trying to sell for a year. We hadn't even advertised it. Someone in the neighborhood just asked about it and we got $1000 for it—ten times my gift to PTL!

J.M.
Richmond, Michigan

UNEXPECTEDLY GETS VAN

In the Spring of this year, we gave for our second Lifetime Partnership. That month, I was given a promotion and substantial raise that more than covered our gift.

This month, we gave for the Silver Membership a $1000 which we were saving to buy a van for our growing family. But on Christmas day, we received a totally unexpected gift of $1500. So, we have the van and the benefits, too.

T.H.
Anderson, Indiana

13

FURNITURE

A NEW JOB AND A NEW STOVE

My son-in-law had been out of a job for almost two and a half years. When you were asking for $1000 Lifetime Partnerships for the new hotel, I sent mine in, and the very next day, he was called to work. The $1000 I sent was money I had saved for a new electric stove for my kitchen. Would you believe that my husband and I found one exactly like I wanted for only $150. Thank the Lord!

Martha Chappel
Marion, Indiana

THINGS FOR HOME PROVIDED

It seems every time I send an offering, something good always comes out of it. I really do believe you have to give to receive.

Like this last time, we were able to sell a riding mower, refrigerator, and wood-burning stove which we weren't using. The money we got is helping us to get some extra things for our new home. God really comes through when we need Him.

Paul Ballinger
Strasburg, Illinois

FURNITURE PROVIDED

Three months ago, I joined PTL as a regular partner. At that time, the only furniture I had was a set of bunk beds.

You should see my home now! I have furniture in every room and even a new washer and dryer. Jesus has provided in so many different ways, more than I could have asked for!

D.B.
Waterford, Michigan

14

EMPLOYMENT

GIVES $1000—RECEIVES NEW JOB WITH COMPANY CAR

I had a job making only $14,000 a year and a car that was falling apart. Since giving $1000 for a Lifetime Membership, God has blessed me with a new job that can pay $30,000 or more a year. I also have a company car to drive. Here is my donation for the Girls' Home and my first payment to become a monthly partner. Thank God for the PTL ministry. It is a blessing to me.

Jack Calderone
Indianapolis, Indiana

LIFETIME, VICTORY, MONTHLY PARTNERS—RAISES AND PROMOTIONS

Since we started pledging to PTL, became Lifetime Members and joined the Victory Club, God has blessed us in many ways too numerous to mention. My husband is supposed to get a review on his job only once a year, but he has received a raise on the average of every six months. He also got a promotion. We give God all the honor and glory.

Bonnie Austin
Douglasville, Georgia

A $1000 INVESTMENT PAYS OFF

After we sent our second Lifetime Partnership, the company which I worked for closed its office in this city. But this was just the thing God used to multiply our pledge. Another company, which is even larger, hired me at a salary thirteen times the amount my partnership cost. All my investments should be that good!

Robert E. Fondren
Wichita, Kansas

LAST TWO DOLLARS YIELDS THREE HUNDRED AND MORE

You challenged me to prove God out of my need, so I sent you my last two dollars and asked God to multiply it back.

I had been out of a job for months but the next day, I got a six-hour job and made $325 that day.

Raymond Gazaway
Bethany, Oklahoma

GETS JOB AFTER SENDING LAST DOLLAR

I was out of work for one year. On May 26th, I called the 800-line for prayer and sent the last dollar I had to help pay the phone bill. On June 6th, I got a check for $400 for overpayment of taxes. Not only that, but I got the best job I ever had in my life.

G.H.
St. Paul, Minnesota

HOUSE SELLS—JOB BLESSING

On April 17th, we sent a check for $1000 to become

124

Lifetime Partners. Just three days later, our house sold!

Three weeks later, my husband was called to work for a company where he'll be making more money than he ever has before, so we can help you more, too.

Betty Akers
Fredericksburg, Virginia

RECEIVE RAISE AFTER BECOMING LIFETIME PARTNERS

We were having financial problems but decided to believe God and gave $1000 to become Lifetime Partners. My husband then received a raise for nearly $5000 a year. God's Word is true: "Give and it shall be given unto you, pressed down, shaken together, and running over."

Andy & Nancy Hoffert
Pottstown, Pennsylvania

SEED FAITH WORKS

I am a double Lifetime Partner. When I sent in for my second Partnership, I seeded faith for a 10% increase in my salary.

Shortly afterward, I got a new job with a 10% increase in pay. God is faithful!

K.M.
Kingsport, Tennessee

JOBS PROVIDED

We joined as PTL Partners earlier this week and sent prayer requests for my husband, Lyle. Just two weeks after Lyle had found the job we had prayed about, he lost it. We were devastated.

We prayed and called PTL. Two days later, a call came through about a job he had been pursuing for a long time. It is wonderful to know God's faithfulness.

Mrs. Lyle Brown
Trenton, Michigan

JOB AND WORK CAR

With my pledge, I sent in two prayer requests. One was for a work car for my husband and the other was for a job. Both have been answered. The job especially because it provides medical insurance and vacation pay.

Mrs. Patsy Jenkins
Turlock, California

STEP OF FAITH LIFETIME MEMBERS—JOB PROMOTION AND RAISE

My husband and I became Lifetime Members even though it looked like his job was going to be discontinued at the time. We stepped out in faith, and Praise The Lord, we did! Two months later, my husband received a promotion with a $100 a week raise. You cannot outgive God!

T.L.
North Carolina

SO BLESSED THAT THEY JOIN THE VICTORY CLUB AGAIN

We were so blessed by joining the Victory Club that

we are sending a separate Victory Club offering. Since joining the first time, my husband got a job, we received an insurance check for $1200, and my husband started his own repair business. There is so much work that he has to turn jobs away. I praise and thank God daily for PTL and count it a privilege to be part of it!

Mrs. Paula Reamer
Clarkston, Michigan

NOT JUST JOB, BUT TOPS IN SALES
Through your prayers, I was able to get this job. Then last month, I was afraid I would lose it because I was at the bottom of the list. But I rebuked Satan and stuck with it, and asked God to bring me through. Today, my boss told me I was the top salesperson this month. God is faithful!

Margaret Flateau
Portmouth, New Hampshire

LIFETIME PARTNER—BETTER JOB FOR SON-IN-LAW
My daughter's husband is a teacher for computer science courses. Summer classes were cancelled because of low enrollment and it was going to be difficult for them to go without this extra income. The week I heard this news, I signed up for a Lifetime Partnership. After two days my daughter called to tell me her husband has summer computer work with a well-established computer firm. It could become a permanent position with a better outlook and future. I gave a membership to PTL

and the Lord gave us back extra employment and extra income. Praise the Lord!

T.C. Steucke
Gerry, New York

VICTORY CLUB VICTORIES

We became members of the Victory Club. The day after we sent in our $125, we got a new car. Five days later, my husband, who had been out of work for two years, received a job.

We had quite a few bills, and two weeks after joining, we received ten times that amount in the mail.

We are rejoicing and are thrilled to be a part of PTL.

Mrs. Emmert Steward
Martingsburg, Pennsylvania

GIVES $10—GETS $10 AN HOUR JOB

The factory where I was employed for the past 10 years closed down. I looked for a new job but couldn't find one. All I could give my wife for her birthday was $10, but instead of buying herself something, she sent the money to PTL. Soon after that, a friend called to tell me about a factory that might be hiring. Over one hundred people had already applied for the job, but I put in my application anyway. I got the job and it pays $10 an hour. God love PTL!

C.H.
McClure, Ohio

JOB AND RAISE IN ONE WEEK

What you have been saying about "Now Is The Time" is true. God is hearing and answering our prayers and blessing our giving.

My husband, Larry, needed a good fulltime job and he was called to it last week. He's already received a raise and gets his first paid holiday this week. After being a self-employed carpenter for the past six years, with off and on work, our home with 5 children really needed stability.

We've grown so much spiritually watching your show and the Lord is beginning to use us to reach others. I do know that it is the Christians' time now!

Wendy Turbyfill
Kentland, Indiana

PART-TIME JOB GIVEN

During the telethon, you said to begin giving at some level. At the time, I was unemployed and barely making it, but I called to give $5 a month and also asked prayer for a job.

Just 2½ hours later, I got a call to start work on a part-time job, which I still have.

G.G.
Sacramento, California

A JOB I REALLY LIKE

Just two days after I sent in $100 to PTL, there was a job cutback at the hospital where I was working and I was laid off. But after just days the Lord opened up a private nursing duty position that I really like.

Christina White
Kingsport, Tennessee

EXTRA WORK

When you challenged us to give in faith, my husband and I were having financial trouble. But we decided to prove God by joining Heritage Club as monthly partners.

Within a few days, my husband started getting extra work. Praise Jesus!

J.H.
Waycross, Georgia

BONUS ON HIS JOB

Yesterday, I called and gave $30 on my credit card to support the People That Love Home. Last night my husband came home with a $600 bonus on his job.

Julie Wilbur
Fort Lauderdale, Florida

NEW BOSS

As PTL Partners, we called PTL to pray for a better situation in my husband's work. His boss was being so rude, due to Larry being a Christian.

That very afternoon, his boss was transferred. His new boss has been a friend for many years.

L.C.
San Antonio, Texas

WORK AFTER 27 MONTH DROUGHT

I had been out of work for 27 months. Two weeks ago I stepped out in faith to become a Partner. Today, I received word that I can go to work tomorrow.

Lewis Wommer
Montgomery, Alabama

JOBS AND JOBS

When I called to join as a Partner, my husband did not have a job. The next day, my husband got a job and within two weeks, he was having to turn jobs down.

C.M
Odessa, Texas

GOD HAD A BETTER PLAN

Since we started giving monthly to PTL, our whole family has really been blessed. I'd been praying and praying about getting a job without success.

Then, in faith, we sent $100 to join the Victory Club. Instead of my getting a job, my husband got a much better one so I could stay home. What a blessing from Jesus!

Mrs. G. A. Jones, III
Chesapeake, Virginia

HOLDING ON

When I sent my December monthly pledge, it was the last of my money. I was out of work and asked prayer for a job.

Praise God, it has happened. I start work next week and will be paid in time for my next monthly pledge.

R.H.
New York, New York

LIFETIME PARTNER FINDS A JOB

I had been unemployed for four years. In faith, I called and pledged $1000 for a Lifetime Partnership. Two days later, I got a job. Praise the Lord! Later I called PTL for prayer for a brother and sister-in-law to be saved. They've both come to know the Lord and were baptized in water.

John Lynch
San Ramon, California

BEST INVESTMENT

On your program, you challenged us to believe God and give in faith, believing God for a miracle. We really needed one, because both my husband and I are out of work and expecting a baby in two months. Well, we called and pledged as monthly partners. Last week, my husband got a job. Praise God! It's the best investment we've ever made.

A.L.
Dayton, Ohio

TRIED IT, IT WORKS

You told me to plant seed and it would be multiplied back to me, but I always thought, "How can I plant when I don't have rent money?" I'd been fired after an extended illness from which I was still recovering. (By the way, I found the Lord while watching your program in the hospital). But still, I decided to send you a tithe from my last check.

Four days later, I found a new job but the work was still too much for me in my condition. I had to quit after three days. But instead of paying me for three days, they paid me for 2 weeks—what a blessing!

Now I've got a new job making $11 an hour, more than I've ever made before.

J.C.
Phoenix, Arizona

BLESSED AT WORK AND WITH FAMILY

Since I gave my first $50 to PTL, marvelous things are happening in my life. First and most important, my oldest son, who is in the Air Force, has been filled with the Holy Spirit.

On my job, I've been blessed with larger tips, more customers, and higher production. I can feel more confident every day!

B.M.
Cabot, Pennsylvania

15

Blessings in Business

GIVES $1000—HAS BEST SELLING MONTH EVER

I run a small used car lot. During the month of May I had my worst month—only four cars sold. It had been on my heart for over a month to give my $1000 for a Lifetime Membership. I sent the $1000 on the first of June. This June I sold the most cars ever in one month. PRAISE THE LORD!

S.M. Patterson
Liberty, North
Carolina

TEN TIMES THE BUSINESS

I own my own business, and as a result of our giving to the Victory Club and Lifetime Partnership, God gave us more business this past May than any May in the history of our business. It was almost 10 times what we did last year in May!

Phil and Chris Gillenwater
Chattanooga, Tennessee

LIFETIME PARTNER—BUSINESS TRIPLES

I just wanted to tell you how very much I love you and P.T.L.

About the same time I became a Lifetime Partner with you, I took the Lord as my business partner. I started praying about *all* things and giving what I hoped to gross from the business.

And in just two months my business has tripled! PRAISE THE LORD!

L.W.
Snellville, Georgia

TWO PARTNERSHIPS—GAIN OWN BUSINESS AND CLOSER-KNIT FAMILY

Three days after we became Lifetime Partners my husband was in a snowmobile accident. After three weeks he was able to return to work, but his job was being done by someone else. My husband was told he would have to work at something he had no experience doing—or else. Things seemed rather gloomy. We had no income whatsoever and had given $1000 of our savings to PTL. PRAISE GOD! He brought us through.

We decided to start our own business and God saw to it that we had enough money to build an office to meet all State specifications and pay all our bills. Then we found ourselves facing a new month of bills with only a few hundred dollars left. We took a second Lifetime Partnership and put it on our charge card. Within hours we received a phone call which resulted in our receiving $3000 in two days. The next day we got several customers which resulted in even more blessings. Not only has God given us this business to support our family, but we have become a closer family unit and are looking to the Lord more than ever for guidance. Thank you for being faithful and being there when there are so many needy souls. Praise the Lord for His goodness and mercy!

> *Ron & Cindy Martin*
> *Wampum, Pennsylvania*

LIFETIME PARTNER/BUSINESS BENEFITS

Sixteen months ago, I gave a faith offering to "Rebuke the Devourer" on behalf of my husband's new satellite antenna business. In the first 12 months, he sold 14 systems!

We then became $1000 Lifetime Partners by putting it on our master card. In less than two months, my husband sold 7 more systems, with 7 more on the verge of saying yes.

Praise the Lord for all He is doing!

> *M.W.*
> *Evans Mills, New York*

CLAIMED VICTORY BUSINESS INCREASED AFTER GIVING

I heard Jim preach on now is the time to go forward and claim victory over satan in our lives. I claimed that for my beauty shop business. It is working.

When I started giving to the PTL Club this year my beauty shop business grossed around $400 to $425 a week. This past week it was right at $800 a week. My goal is $1000 a week. I work by myself but the Lord is opening the door for me to have a part-time assistant. Praise His Name!

> *Mrs. M.R. Hendrick*
> *Greenville, Mississippi*

GIVING IS GOOD BUSINESS

Our business was failing. We sent money to PTL and the very next day business began to boom. Not only did it double that week, but we also received a check for $284!

B.G.
Denham Springs, Louisiana

$2 MILLION IN SALES

I Sent $1000 to PTL to become a Lifetime Partner—Two weeks later, I sold one million dollars in insurance.

We decided to send another $1000 today for another Lifetime Partnership! God Bless You All!

Robert Cade
Arlington, Texas

MY HUSBAND NOW HAS THRIVING BUSINESS

My husband Peter and I were having very serious financial difficulties. Peter's business partner had stolen thousands of dollars and betrayed him to a point almost beyond endurance. Not only was the business in a helpless state, but we had just bought a home and I had chosen to quit work to take care of our new baby.

It was about this time we began watching PTL. When you held your telethon we were down to accepting meals at our in-laws and existing on homemade soup for weeks at a time. However, we did as you said and stepped out in faith. We pledged $1000 and became $15 monthly partners. We also began giving to ten other Christian organizations and gave away things we no longer needed in our home. We decided to concentrate on others' needs and expected a miracle.

It worked! My husband now has a thriving business, our finances are in top shape, and bills no longer threaten to destroy our lives. We are free!

Anyone who doesn't believe this or use it for themselves is missing so much. It works!

M.M.
Spring Lake Park, Minnesota

GOD REBUKED THE DEVOURER

My wife and I own and operate a service station/car wash. While other stations are going under all around us, our cup is running over. Through our regular support of PTL over the past 3 years, we have become Lifetime Partners four times.

Through unjust means, the large oil company that we lease from tried to terminate our lease and take the station. Reminded of what you said that God would rebuke the devourer if we give, we just got down on our knees and prayed, asking God to solve the problem and then went to work.

Sure enough, the oil company phoned and announced they had changed their mind and were giving us back the station.

L.B. Evans
Clackamas, Oregon

TRUST IN GOD REPAYS LOAN FOR
LIFETIME PARTNERSHIP

My husband and I went to the bank and borrowed $1000 for a Lifetime Partnership. We didn't know how on earth we could pay it back, but we put our faith into God's hands. A few weeks later, my husband received a check in the mail for $906.88 from his employer. He had turned in a suggestion at work which had originally been turned down . . . But now he was being notified that it had been accepted after all!

I thank God for helping us get the money to pay back our loan.

I know you can and will make it because the PTL ministry has changed my life.

> Betty Smith
> Morrow, Georgia

GOD FIGHTS BATTLE

God does fight our battles and rebukes the devourer! The month after we came to PTL and gave $1000 for our Lifetime Partnership we received a check in the mail for $2900. It came from a man who had not made good on a business deal long before this.

> F.A.
> Calhoun, Kentucky

TWO LIFETIME PARTNERSHIPS—TWO BLESSINGS

We gave $2,000 for two Lifetime Partnerships. My husband gave $1000 through his company and I gave $1000 of my own. Before we left for vacation we prayed over our house, asking God to protect it and keep it safe. We enjoyed our vacation but God led us to come home two days early. When we got home, we discovered that our home had been broken into. The thieves were in the house when the garage door lifted and fled when they heard us coming. Not one thing was taken. The thieves did not even take anything on the way out. In our case God kept the devourer from taking fifty times over the $1000 amount I gave. Also, there was a check in the mail to my husband's company from the IRS for $4000 in overpaid taxes. My husband gave through his company and the company was blessed four times over. PRAISE GOD FOR HIS BLESSINGS!

> JRH
> Odessa, Texas

RECEIVES NEEDED MACHINERY

When we were at PTL, we planted a seed of $225 for a $22,500 piece of machinery for our business. Before we even got home, the machinery was on its way to us. You can't out-give God.

> Dot & Sam Stanton
> Chipley, Florida

SMALL BUSINESS DOUBLES

Since we sent the gift for our Lifetime Partnership, my small business has more than doubled. To be able to stay at the beautiful Grand Hotel is icing on the cake—the $1000 was given to God. We agreed if we never got to Heritage USA to use it, it would be fine. God has blessed us.

> L.R.
> Morgantown, Tennessee

16

MARRIAGES & FAMILIES RESTORED & BLESSED

MARRIAGE RESTORED AND JOB PROVIDED

My husband had just left me and I didn't know what I'd do. Sending PTL that last $25, I didn't know when or how I would get some more money.

However, it wasn't more than 10 minutes after I returned from the Post Office that I received a call to start work the next day. Two weeks later, my husband returned to my baby and me. Our home is healed and God has helped us pay our bills and give to PTL.

Rosalind Brown
Ozark, Alabama

FAMILY RICHLY BLESSED AFTER PLEDGING $1000

By faith I pledged $1000 to become a Lifetime Partner, and God has been blessing me! There is more harmony in my family now. My husband is so wonderful to me. My son is home again and my two married daughters will be giving us our first grandchildren this year. To top it all, I received the money someone owed me. The last payment was

143

not due until 1987, but I got it in a lump sum of close to $6000. Praise God, Praise God!

Maria A. Condon
Brandon, Florida

FRIEND'S MARRIAGE HEALED

Thank you for your prayers for our Victory Club requests. The first answer came the same day I sent to PTL—our three year old had had an earache for two weeks and the morning he was completely healed. We also requested prayer for some friend's marriage, who had been talking about divorce. The next week, the husband came to church with us for the first time.

Rose Bulske
Dearborn, Michigan

HUSBAND AWAKENS BY VISIT TO PTL

Last year, I was the only Spirit-filled person at home. Then my husband and I went to PTL. Wow! A fire was lit in my husband that was never there before. He wanted to become a Lifetime Partner before I even asked him! We are also members of the Victory Club and want to tell you we are behind PTL 100%!

Mrs. W. Bruns
Buffalo Grove, Illinois

HUSBAND SAVED, MARRIAGE BLESSED

I came to know Jesus as my Savior watching your program eight years ago. And I have been praying for my husband's salvation ever since.

He always thought television was phony, so I had to save for a long time a little personal money to become a Lifetime Partner. When it came time to use it to come to Heritage USA, he decided he would come along with me.

Well, the pastor in the Upper Room prayed for him. He was saved; then got baptized in water at the hotel; he was healed of a severe eye condition; and we went to the marriage workshops and received a miracle in our marriage.

He bought a second Lifetime Partnership before we left.

B.P.
Naples, Florida

HUSBAND DELIVERED FROM CIGARETTES

This is our 17th wedding anniversary, and as a token of our love to you and to God, we are enclosing a check for $100. We are casting our vote for victory by joining the Victory Club.

My husband is there with you working on the Grand Hotel, and I will be joining him soon. The very first day he was there and walked into the Upper Room, THE HOLY SPIRIT TOOK AWAY ALL DESIRE FOR CIGARETTES. We really praise the Lord, because my husband had tried so hard to quit . . . but there is nothing too hard for God.

W.T.
Toronto, Ohio

MARRIAGE BLESSED BY GIVING

I discovered PTL during a very low point in my life. Within four months, I became a partner, sent $100 for the Parallel Bible, gave $25 to help support the TV stations, and joined the Lifetime Partnership. My husband never once gave me a hard time about sending money, even though he was concerned about our money situation. But we are doing great and our bills are getting paid. Although we have not had a tenfold or even a twofold dollar return, the Lord has given us much more. I thank God every day for my husband, because I know that God gave us to each other. We look at each other more as a gift from God and I feel that we are less selfish and more compassionate than ever before. We really are blessed. Thank you for being there for us.

Sharon Khula
Mt. Clemens, Michigan

HUSBAND SAVED—MANY BLESSINGS

I started watching PTL about four years ago. It took my husband a little while longer, but it was your program that brought him to the Lord.

This year, he cashed in a bond to buy us a Lifetime Partnership. When we came, it was the best vacation we ever had. In the Upper Room, I was healed of chest pains.

To top it off, when we got home, I had a check for $3000 waiting from an inheritance from a distant relative. So we got another Partnership. You can't out-give God!

E.N.
Norwood, Ohio

A LIFE AND HOME SAVED

Your message came straight to me at the right time. My home and marriage was in such a mess, I was contemplating taking a gun to kill myself.

When I heard you speak on just the way I felt, I called the prayer line and knew then that I could make it with God's help. I'm sending you a tithe to believe God with me for total healing of my marriage.

S.B.
Milford, Ohio

I TOOK FOUR!

I took four Lifetime Partnerships for my four children. Did I receive a blessing from the Lord when I found out my oldest son was voted "Father of the Year!

Geneva Cuthrell
Fort Mill, South Carolina

MARRIAGE HEALED

Since receiving Christ through your broadcast and joining PTL as a Partner in April, God has healed my broken marriage and saved my husband's soul as well. I can't tell you how much this means to me.

W.W.
Stevensville, Montana

FAMILY AND OUTLOOK IMPROVED 100%

I've been watching your show for the last six months and it has changed my life! Although I was brought up in a Christian home, a tragedy had caused me to doubt the goodness and love of God.

Then I saw your program and four months ago, I became a regular monthly Partner. Since that time, God has improved my life, my family situation, and my outlook by more than 100%.

M.D.
Fresno, California

GIVEN ONE TO CARE

This month, I'm sending an extra $25 for the First Aid Kit To Victory. God has been giving me victory since I first started my monthly pledge.

God has ended my loneliness and given me a nice Christian man who cares. Praise God!

B.H.
Berwick, Maine

MARRIAGE BETTER

My husband and I just recently became PTL monthly Partners and ever since that time our marriage has been better and God has truly shone a bright light of hope into our lives. I just received your set of "The Fixed Laws Of God" and oh, how my life so desperately needed to be filled with these messages. Now I know that faith without works is impossible.

E.M.
Fayetteville, North Carolina

LOVED ONE RETURNED AND SAVED

For two years, as a young child, Mike lived with us

as a foster child. Then he returned to his mother, who is a lesbian.

For eight years, we'd been praying for his welfare. We sent PTL $1000 as seed faith for victory. Just recently, Mike's mother called to give us guardianship of Mike. He's come back, been saved, received the baptism of the Holy Spirit, and is witnessing to his mother.

J.H.
Fair Oaks, California

GRANDDAUGHTER RETURNED

With our Victory Club offering was a prayer request for the return of our granddaughter who had run away from home. Yesterday, my daughter-in-law called to say that she had returned home, safe and sound.

R.D.
Lockwood, New York

17

SALVATIONS

JOINS VICTORY CLUB—TWO SONS SAVED
I am a single parent of five children. Since I sent in
$50 towards the Victory Club my two sons, thirteen
and eight years old, gave their lives to the Lord.

> *Phyllis Duhart*
> *Little Rock, Arkansas*

MOTHER FINDS NEW LIFE THROUGH PTL
I'm 39 years old, married, and have 3 daughters. I
have not been the mother or the wife I should, or
could be. I was always too busy finding wrong in
others and didn't take time for my family.

I drank, smoked pot, and when I thought I was
too tired I would pop a pill. It made life unbearable,
not only for me, but for my family also.

I knew I needed something in my life, but just
what, I didn't know. Then one day, about 4 months
ago, I was watching television and a Christian program came on and a woman named Tammy looked
right at me and said, "Now is the time for you.
Jesus loves you. He wants you to be happy. He will
take care of your problems. Just say, 'Jesus, I'm
yours.'"

That morning, I prayed like I've never prayed

before and right then, Jesus came into my heart and my life. He will stay there forever.

I love you both and so does my family!

A.B.
Santa Ana, California

TESTIMONY FROM 11 YEAR OLD BOY

I'm eleven years old and I've been watching your show from ten years old until now. I enjoy watching your show and I thank you for teaching me about God.

I saw the show where you read the letter about the lady who thought she sinned so badly that she could never be forgiven. I thought that way too . . . until I saw that show. Now I'm up and fighting the war for Jesus!

I hope you will stay on the air for a long time, because I still have a lot more to learn.

Todd Hamilton
St. Paul, Minnesota

SAVED INSTEAD OF SOAPS

By the grace of God and Christian television I am born again and a new creature in Christ. Several months ago, I had never seen your show and was in deep depression, was on a drinking binge and considered suicide as the only way out of my loneliness.

Somehow on this particular day, as I turned on the TV to see the "soaps" a preacher was saying "God loves you, He really does." I wanted to change the channel but for some reason I couldn't. I watched your entire program.

Then another Christian program came on and the host had a word of knowledge that someone was in deep depression and thinking of suicide. God's Spirit hit me and I fell to my knees. My life was instantly changed! I praise our Lord every day for all He has done.

By the way, the "soaps" no longer hold any of my attention. Neither does loneliness. I'm too busy reading my Bible and learning what God wants me to do. I want everyone to have this great miracle of life!

H.W.
Only, Tennessee

SON SAVED AND DELIVERED

I gave $100 in faith for victory for my son. It has happened. He is now in a treatment center for alcoholism. The devil is defeated in his life, and can no longer control his mind through drugs.

Greg has become a born again, spirit-filled young man.

N.B.
Reno, Nevada

A DOUBLE VICTORY BLESSING

I received Jesus Christ through PTL and joined the Victory Club. Within one week, my 16 year old daughter came home from church and announced, through tears, that she had been saved. Also, within ten days, God prompted someone to deposit $1500 into my bank account. Thank the Lord!

Evelyn Inderhitzer
Modesto, California

CHILDREN SAVED

Since I joined PTL as a monthly Partner, God is blessing in such a great way. My four children and their families are now saved, attending church and working for Jesus.

L.P.
Gadsen, Alabama

HUSBAND SAVED

I planted a seed of $100 for my husband to come to Jesus.

He has come to the Lord and is now watching your program and reading the Bible.

M.M.
Lee Center, New York

SAVED AND DELIVERED

Since I sent my first payment for the Victory Club, God has changed my life. I had been into heavy abuse of alcohol and drugs. I had no job, no money, and no place to go. Then my sister and brother-in-law took me in and gave me shelter. They kept telling me about Jesus and gradually it got through to me. Two weeks after receiving Jesus, I found a well paying job in my favorite type of work. I've now received two raises and a new motorcycle.

S.S.
Middleton, Indiana

HUSBAND SAVED—HUNDREDFOLD BLESSING

When we visited Heritage USA we gave a seed faith offering of $125. We returned home and the next week were able to sell a vehicle and trailer for $12,500, making us debt free for the first time in many years. God returned our seed faith a hundredfold.

We are Lifetime Partners and God has given back many times already. But the best part is my husband is now saved and our family is coming together again.

B.K.
Lancaster, Ohio

BECOMES LIFETIME PARTNER

Approximately two weeks ago, while searching for an alternative to the Johnny Carson Show, I tuned in WCFC, Channel 38 in Chicago and there you were! I watched your show for a few minutes and then switched channels again, but nothing seemed to satisfy me, so I switched back to your show. Since that night, I've become a regular viewer.

It has been nearly 30 years since I had Jesus in my life, but thanks to you and Tammy, and the guests you've had on your show, you've brought Him back into my life once again. Enclosed please find our check, in the amount of $1000, so that we may become Lifetime Partners. Also, please count us as regular monthly Partners.

I've never felt so strongly about anything, except that your TV show has to keep reaching new and lost souls.

R.R.
Bristol, Wisconsin

18

HEALINGS

GAVE GENEROUSLY—RECEIVED TWO MIRACLE HEALINGS

I have sent two Lifetime Partnerships, two Victory Club memberships, plus several donations to PTL. Since giving to PTL, I was healed of a serious vision problem and a painful back problem. I praise God every day for my two miracles and all my blessings. God loves you and I do too!

Blanche Pride
Colonial Heights, Virginia

EYESIGHT RESTORED AFTER JOINING VICTORY CLUB

I was watching PTL one day and you, Jim, were talking about the Girls' Home. I couldn't afford it then, but I felt so strongly about this Home that I mailed in my first $25 for the Victory Club. For the past twelve to fifteen years I had to wear glasses for my poor eyesight. The Lord blessed me by totally restoring my eyes. I can see leaves on trees, grass on hills, and colours so vividly it doesn't seem real. You can't put a price on perfect eyesight. I can't even drive down the road without shedding tears of joy. Our Lord is so wonderful! I am praying and believing together with PTL.

Shari Haumann
Thedford, Nebraska

HUSBAND HEALED OF LOW BLOOD PRESSURE

My husband and I sent a check for $1000 for the Heritage Grand Hotel. We sent it out of desperation because we had so many doctor bills. Shortly afterward, we received a totally unexpected check for three times as much! My husband also had a problem with low blood pressure and dizziness, and had been on several different kinds of medication. I took him for a check-up and told the doctor he could walk alone and do things he couldn't do before. The doctor checked his blood pressure, heart, and lungs, and said, "It's a miracle!"

Mildred Chase
Richmond, Virginia

SON HEALED FROM HEADACHES

Being a PTL Partner means so much. When my son was having regular bad headaches that were keeping him from working regularly, I knew that it was an attack from Satan.

So I called PTL and asked the prayer counselor to agree in prayer that Satan would be bound in this situation. Since that very day, he has had no more headaches and has not missed work. In fact, he's making overtime.

Ida Redding
LaPorte, Indiana

VICTORY OVER SKIN CANCER

I called PTL for prayer for my husband who had skin cancer all over his face. I also sent in my $100 to join the Victory Club. The cancer fell right off his face! Praise God for His healing power!

Mrs. Furman Bishop
Rome, Georgia

DAUGHTER'S EYES HEALED

When my daughter, Tara, was born, she was born without eyeballs. The doctors told me she could either have her eyelids sewn shut or have glass eyeballs.

My grandmother called the PTL prayer line, and today, Tara has neither glass eyes nor sewn lids—she has "miniature eyeballs" and has useful vision. The doctors are totally amazed.

She lives almost a perfectly normal life. Through the prayers of the PTL people, I know that God answered this prayer.

K.H.
Oak Hill, Ohio

HEALED OF PROSTATE CANCER

On April 24, I found out I had cancer of the prostate. We're monthly partners so my wife called PTL for prayer for my healing.

On May 16th, I had an extensive biopsy. I told the Doctor that the Lord had healed me of all cancer and he would find nothing. The next day, I was told that absolutely no cancer had been found.

Edward Nickel
South Point, Ohio

CANCER HEALING

I am so happy to be a PTL Partner today! Just weeks ago, life looked so black. That was when the doctor told my husband that he was dying of cancer and emphysema.

We called PTL and prayed with the Upper Room prayer counselor for a miracle. Then we went back to a specialist who examined my husband, said the cancer was treatable and he could live at least ten more healthy years and sent my husband back to work. PTL!

R. & H. L.
E. Detroit, Michigan

SON PROTECTED AND HEALED

Until recently, I did not know the importance of giving faithfully to the Lord's work. Although I am on a small fixed income supporting three sons, I have been beginning to give faithfully, believing God for His provision.

And He has provided—in every way. Last Thursday, my son was hit in the mouth by a heavy steel bar from the back of a truck. Miraculously, the doctors were able to save all his teeth and he didn't have any fractures or permanent damage.

I know God intervened as I prayed and bound the destroyer, asking God for His mercy.

Barbara Hill
Hollidaysburg, Pennsylvania

HEALING OF DOWNE'S SYNDROME

Last month, after we sent our monthly offering, I called you to pray for our 2 month old daughter born with Downe's Syndrome. Ten days ago, the doctors confirmed that she is completely healed.

D.W.
Vancouver, Washington

LIFETIME PARTNER BACK ON FEET AGAIN

Ever since my husband and I became Lifetime Partners, wonderful things have happened. I have had Multiple Sclerosis since 1971. I was in a wheelchair for the last three years. The Lord has taken the pain out of my back and legs and put me back on my feet. I can now walk about 44 feet with a walker. I can and will make it with the help of the Lord. Praise His name!

Ray Sweigart
Mount Joy, Pennsylvania

LIFETIME PARTNERSHIP—SON-IN-LAW GETS JOB—MOM PROTECTED FROM FALL

My mother gave us $1000 to join the Lifetime Partnerships. With my check I sent a prayer request for my son-in-law to get a job. He was out of work for nearly a year. Praise Jesus! He got a real good job with terrific pay only 5 minutes from home.

But that is not all. My mother, who is eighty-six, fell down flights of stairs and landed on cement. She was carrying a glass plate and she landed in the broken glass. She did not get one scratch and not one broken bone. The doctor could not believe it and made her take more X-rays. He read them for 1½ hours and still could not find a single fracture.

Everybody says this is a miracle. The Lord truly intervened. Praise His holy name!

Helen Seykoski
Monessen, Pennsylvania

DAUGHTER HEALED

God is performing miracles in my life since becoming a PTL Partner. I called PTL for prayer for my seven-year-old daughter who had a skin type lupus. There is no known cure for lupus, but the phone counselor told me to anoint her with oil. I did this and the pain left her immediately. I took her to the doctor and he said the scars are disappearing and there are no traces of lupus.

P.R.
Casar, North Carolina

HEALING AND FINANCIAL BLESSING

My husband was sick with stomach ulcers for $1^1/2$ years. One day, while watching PTL, you, Jim, said there is a woman who is crying and doesn't know what to do because her husband is sick with stomach ulcers. You told me to give it all up to God and that he would deliver my husband in three weeks. Three weeks right to the day my husband decided to go with me to church and was instantly healed and born again. That week the doctor had planned to remove his stomach and he couldn't understand how my husband's stomach was like brand new. That was all back in 1978. This year, since we gave $1000 for a Lifetime Partnership, our business has tripled. My husband has had to turn away contractors. Praise God!

M.T.
Leicester, Massachusetts

HEALED OF BREAST CANCER AFTER WORD OF KNOWLEDGE

I found a mass in my breast. No hope was given that it wouldn't be cancer. I called PTL for prayer. That night I was watching the program and you, Jim had a word of knowledge. You said not to worry and that everything was going to be all right. I received that for me and the next day there was no mass and no cancer. God is with me!

Margaret Miller
Lancaster, Pennsylvania

MIRACULOUS RECOVERY

Recently, my husband had me send in for two Lifetime Partnerships. Within a few days, he was notified at work of being given a $1000 a month raise effective the first of the previous month, which meant our $2000 gift was returned almost immediately.

Also, we had sent in a prayer request for my husband's father who had a severe stroke. He began to improve immediately and is now home. The doctors call it a "miraculous recovery."

D.V.
Springfield, Missouri

HOSPITAL PAID BILL AFTER JOINING VICTORY CLUB

Last September, the doctor told me I had a large cancerous mass on my left ovary. My family prayed for me. On the day I had surgery, the doctor was stunned. The cancer was gone! However, he removed a large abcess from my colon and I was left with $4,463.50 in hospital bills and no insurance to cover it. I applied for help at the welfare department, but was denied.

In May of this year, I joined the Victory Club. The next month, I got a notice that my application had been re-evaluated and welfare would pay every bit of the bill. Praise the Lord!

Joyce Fogle
Lebanon, Indiana

HEALING AND FINANCIAL BLESSING

I praise God for answers for prayer. Shortly after I became pregnant, I began to have trouble. I was told by my doctor three times that my baby would never be born.

But I telephoned the Upper Room constantly for prayer during my pregnancy, and six days ago, my healthy baby girl was born.

As a praise offering and a special thank you for your prayers, I gave a $5000 gift to PTL. The very next day, I received a $25,000 inheritance from a relative.

K.J.
Troy, Michigan

CRUSHED LEG IS TOTALLY HEALED

One morning, I was looking for cartoons on the TV when my son came across Tammy Faye singing, "Now Is The Time." Then, Jim, you said there was someone out there who was ready for a healing now.

My brother-in-law had a 5000-pound lathe fall on his leg. It was so badly smashed that he had to have numerous operations and an abundance of pins put into his bones. He was not even allowed to stand on his leg because the doctors were afraid it would crumble. I put my hand on the TV and prayed for him to be healed. That afternoon, he called all excited. The doctor couldn't believe what the X-rays showed! My brother-in-law is now walking on his own two legs with no therapy! Thank you for claiming the victory with us!

Mrs. James McConnell
York, Pennsylvania

HEALING OF PAST HURTS

The first of this month, I got cable TV and started watching your daily program. At the time, I was very discouraged and was getting things in order to commit suicide!

But hearing Tammy sing "Now Is The Time" made me feel that perhaps there is a future for me.

I still have a lot of hurts from the past where I've let the devil and others tear me down. But daily, your program lifts me up and helps me release the past to Jesus and look to God's goodness for the day. Yes, Now Is The Time to look to God and join PTL.

M.F.
Portland, Oregon

HEALED FROM BURNS

On May 22, I was severely burned when my oven exploded. My right hand was a mass of blisters.

I called PTL at 5:30 a.m. for prayer. On May 23, my hand had no burns and no blisters. I was totally healed.

Blanche Swegles
Raritan, New Jersey

CALLED PTL FOR PRAYER FOR SON'S EYE SURGERY

Back in February, my son had an accident at school with a pencil. The point was shoved in just above the eyeball, but the X-rays showed nothing. Three days later, the eye swelled shut and after two months, it was no better. He complained of headaches so severe he could not see.

The doctors ran every test they could for over three weeks. They still couldn't find anything wrong. Finally, he was taken to a hospital for a CAT scan that showed something in the brain. On May 18th, my son went into surgery. I called PTL for prayers. I felt the Lord's comfort and peace all through me. I knew he was in control of the operation.

After $4\frac{1}{2}$ hours, the doctor came out and told us he had to remove a $\frac{1}{2}$ inch piece of pencil lead and lots of infection. As soon as this was done, the brain returned to normal.

Today, my son is as the Lord promised—100% normal. I want to thank the Lord and all of PTL!

L. S.
Mansfield, Ohio

STOMACH ULCERS HEALED AFTER MAILING IN PRAYER REQUESTS

My sister-in-law had stomach ulcers for quite some time. I sent in a prayer request to PTL for her healing. The request was sent on Saturday and on the following Monday, she went to the hospital for tests. Her ulcers were all healed. God does work miracles.

J.S.
Milroy, Pennsylvania

MOM HEALED AFTER CALLING PTL FOR PRAYER

My mother was very sick and weak. She went to the doctor but he could not help her at all. When we went to the grocery store, she couldn't even carry her groceries from the car to her house. As a monthly partner, I called PTL for prayer.

Since then, she went to see another doctor and he couldn't find anything wrong with her. She is stronger and even went out to mow the lawn. Praise the Lord for His healing power.

Also, the Lord has blessed us so much financially that I am sending an extra $50 in addition to my monthly pledge this month.

Peggy Fisher
Flint, Michigan

WORD OF KNOWLEDGE FOR MOM WITH BABY

One day I was watching PTL and Tammy had a word of knowledge. While singing "Now Is The Time," she told a mother that her baby in the crib is healed and then went on to explain about a white sink and a mother's frustration. The day before, my baby had fallen underneath the sink and cut himself. He also had a cold and a terrible cough. He's sleeping now and I believe he is healed and that Jesus lives in this home. We are blessed with your program and are enclosing a check for $15. Faith will lead you where reason can't walk!

Cyndi Hughes
Great Falls, Montana

WOMAN HEALED OF LEUKEMIA

You have no idea what PTL means to me! Within the last three years, I have spoken to prayer counselors at PTL about three times because my mother was extremely ill.

Well, praise God! Due to you at PTL agreeing with me in prayer, my mother has been gloriously and completely healed of leukemia. She will be 66 years old in a few weeks and has been completely healed by God's grace.

Thank you for building an organization—more like a family—that is there in the middle of the night to respond to the cry of one small person like me.

S.N.
Bronx, New York

168

19

CHURCHES BLESSED

OFFERING COMES BACK
I was impressed that our church was to send $1000 to PTL. When I shared this in church, the offering was 2$\frac{1}{2}$ times the largest offering we ever had before.

Rev. Sam Holloway
Memphis, Tennessee

NEW CHURCH BUILDING AND NEW HOME
I just want to tell you of a beautiful blessing that my husband, who is a Pastor, I and our congregation received from the Lord, that you and your team helped to pray for.

Last year, 1983, we were trying to get a loan on a church building. It was a rather slow process, because we did not have a sufficient down payment.

I mailed you, with my husbands' consent, $100 toward your work as seed faith.

I didn't ask for anything from you, because we just wanted the Lord to bless the loan to go through. However, you sent us a Parallel Bible, for which we're very grateful to you. I enjoy it very much.

Thank God, on March 31, 1984, we moved into

our new building. The Lord also added a bonus by giving us a home also, all in one.

Delores Johnson
San Francisco, California

CHURCH THRIVING AFTER BECOMING PTL CENTER

Ever since our church joined your effort as a local People That Love Center, we have really been thriving. Daily people are coming to know the love of God, friends and the community.

The whole Christian community is getting behind our center with food drives, yard sales, donations and benefits to help us. The Lord is adding many to the church. Many of our Center volunteers, too, have found a new sense of direction and purpose in their Christian walk.

Rev. Farina
Greenville, Pennsylvania

LOVE CENTER TEACHES CHURCH TO BATTLE SATAN

God is blessing our new People That Love Center. It has really put our people to work and souls are being won to Christ. They are learning to battle Satan instead of one another. What a blessing!

Rev. Richard Brown
Tarpon Springs, Florida

CHURCH GROWS BY HELPING POOR

Reaching the poor for Christ through your People That Love Center strategy is the best means I've ever tried for church growth. In two months, we have served 431 families, had 27 conversions, 2 healings, and 7 filled with the Holy Spirit. God is working miracles there every day.

N.A.
Mankato, Minnesota

HELPING POOR BRINGS UNITY AND PROSPERITY

God is building unity and bringing prosperity to the whole body of Christ here, since our church became a local People That Love Center to help the poor. We have been working with several inner-city church to help these people get the clothing and shoes they need. We provided one church over 100 sets of clothing and shoes.

In return, God provided our church with a car we really needed. Our people are seeing what's happening and catching the spirit of giving. It's beautiful.

Rev. K. Davis
Fort Wayne, Indiana

FINDS GOOD CHURCH

When I first joined as a monthly Partner, I sent with it a prayer request to find a good church in my area. I wanted one that believed and preached like you.

That week, a woman walked into the utilities office where I work and blurted out that God had heard my cry and would take care of the problem. At first, I thought she was kooky, but we became friends and she helped me find a beautiful church to attend in nearby Duluth.

D.S.
Norcross, Georgia